MEDICAL
INTIMACY

DEEPER UNDERSTANDING ALLOWS
FOR DEEPER HEALING

DR. CHARLES D. CORAM

BALBOA
PRESS
A DIVISION OF HAY HOUSE

Copyright © 2017 Dr. Charles D. Coram.

All rights reserved. No part of this book may be used or reproduced by any means, graphic, electronic, or mechanical, including photocopying, recording, taping or by any information storage retrieval system without the written permission of the author except in the case of brief quotations embodied in critical articles and reviews.

Balboa Press books may be ordered through booksellers or by contacting:

Balboa Press
A Division of Hay House
1663 Liberty Drive
Bloomington, IN 47403
www.balboapress.com
1 (877) 407-4847

Because of the dynamic nature of the Internet, any web addresses or links contained in this book may have changed since publication and may no longer be valid. The views expressed in this work are solely those of the author and do not necessarily reflect the views of the publisher, and the publisher hereby disclaims any responsibility for them.

The author of this book does not dispense medical advice or prescribe the use of any technique as a form of treatment for physical, emotional, or medical problems without the advice of a physician, either directly or indirectly. The intent of the author is only to offer information of a general nature to help you in your quest for emotional and spiritual well-being. In the event you use any of the information in this book for yourself, which is your constitutional right, the author and the publisher assume no responsibility for your actions.

Any people depicted in stock imagery provided by Thinkstock are models, and such images are being used for illustrative purposes only.
Certain stock imagery © Thinkstock.

Print information available on the last page.

ISBN: 978-1-5043-7522-1 (sc)
ISBN: 978-1-5043-7524-5 (hc)
ISBN: 978-1-5043-7523-8 (e)

Library of Congress Control Number: 2017903069

Balboa Press rev. date: 03/10/2017

Dedication

This book is dedicated to my wife, Brenda; my three amazing children, Addison, Mercedes, and Olivia. Without their love, support, and patience this book would never of been born.

Acknowledgements

I am deeply grateful to Kathy Hansen-Butler, who was instrumental in the conception, formulation and writing of this book, for her creativity, her ability to put abstract ideas into words, and her willingness to explore with me in depth the underlying mechanics of the process of healing.

I extend my gratitude to Susanna McCan, for her editing and publishing skills, brillant feedback, and depth of understanding.

To all the readers who gave me outstanding feedback, which guided and shaped this final book. Special thanks, to Michael McKay, a true friend. To Rosemary Vandello, for her meticulous mind.

With all my gratitude, I thank these wonderful souls who came into my life and shared with me their stories of suffering and difficulties. These stories fill the pages with the miraculous ability that we all have to withstand great challenges and to overcome unimaginable adversity.

Foreword

It is my great privilege to write a foreword to exalt the true value of Medical Intimacy.

This book is a quintessential guide for everyone who has ever wondered how healing happens or has a desire to empower and encourage others or themselves in what is possible in the realm of healing. MY greatest intention is to inspire YOU to not only study this book for every nugget and nuance you might glean, but also to share it far and wide.

At this tumultuous time in our world, more than ever, we seek touchstones to know it is possible to experience hope, wonder, and inspiration. Medical Intimacy offers an opportunity to explore the essential elements for mastery in renewing balance in living systems through conscious engagement with inner life experiences and Healing Presence. This is not a conceptual exploration. Medical Intimacy is a journey into living stories that engage every aspect of you and these stories will inspire you and restore hope!

The insights by Dr. Coram and the individual experiences shared within these pages express nuances of perception available only when we access the multiple intelligences of our body, heart, mind, and soul in alignment with a Greater Power. The experience of union between Divine Awareness combined with the physical, mental, and emotional manifestation of health, wholeness, and healing is beautifully documented here in ways that will take you deeper into self-awareness.

It is an honor to acknowledge the clarity of Dr. Charles Coram in how he communicates creating an environment for healing and the demonstrations that have been hallmark of his work. Dr. Coram invites a fertile receptivity where well-being and return to wholeness emerges according to the natural laws of the universe. He does this through his innate awareness, willingness to listen deeply to internal wisdom, loving acceptance, and attention to the body knowledge of his clients. In this loving field of Presence, or as today's scientists might describe, in this quantum field of pure potential, there is access to freedom from suffering, pain, and fear.

The powerful, life-affirming testimonies within Medical Intimacy acknowledge the full-spectrum freedom that is experienced by Dr. Coram's patients. These clients achieve the results of a transformed life at every level-not just physical, but also a mental, emotional, and spiritual freedom that creates happy, fulfilled and expanded living. This is hugely significant in our world that hungers to be free from the clutches of daily and life-long suffering. Here the clients and all who would follow this pathway find an effective holistic whole-Being approach to healing and wellness that leads them from a life of fear-avoidance to fuller self-expression, clarity, and ease in living.

The moment I met Dr. Charles Coram, I had an instant recognition of another healing presence, a high vibration, consciously awake and aware soul here to transform the world. My mother experienced relief from excruciating pain that no one else had been able to relieve through countless surgeries, therapies and medications. She also found an inner peace that had been eluding her throughout her entire life.

Dr. Coram is also a highly respected colleague of my brother, who at that time was a neurologist for the area. My own experience was a deep inner harmony and unraveling of tensions. I felt such movement within me through our exchange that I wrote to acknowledge my gratitude for the experiences that blessed me on all levels of my being. Dr. Coram helps his patients see that they are not "broken" but a beautiful expression of the perfect pattern of life that is revealed as they open to their Essence.

Dr. Charles Coram's seminal book is important to all in the world. Through the study of this book, you too will gain the wisdom to experience the true pattern of wholeness and how to access it through Dr. Coram's sensitive, informative, and inspired writing.

As you engage your own journey through the pages of Medical Intimacy, may you access this dynamic consciousness within yourself and also be inspired to support others in their own empowerment and healing.

In Loving Gratitude and Oneness,

Reverend Kyra Baehr
Minister, Unity Bay Area Houston,
Oneness Trainer and Spiritual Coach
League City, Texas

Contents

Dedication v

Acknowledgements vii

Foreword ix

Introduction xv

Chapter 1 Curing the Incurable: The Basics of
           Medical Intimacy 1

Chapter 2 Giving Back Hope 7

Chapter 3 Edges—A Space Where Miracles Are Born 12

Chapter 4 Setting Our Intentions: Consciously
           Examining the Role of Intention in Healing 19

Chapter 5 Dissolving Self-Destructive Patterns—
           Shifting Attention to the Health of the
           Whole System 36

Chapter 6 Merging With Our Source—Expanding
           Our Perspective 42

Chapter 7 The Power of Trust—Another Referral 57

Chapter 8 A Sense of Relief—Pointing Us in the
           Right Direction for Healing 64

Chapter 9 Fear—The Elephant in the Room 73

Chapter 10 Uniqueness—Finding Our Own Path 86

Chapter 11 The God Finder—Tying It All Together 98

Introduction

For years, both colleagues and patients have asked me to write a book about my unique approach to healing. The big question is, with the field of medicine so vast these days, why do patients find my work unique?

To start with, the whole focus of my healing practice has been *to help patients who are seeking to heal themselves*—to support my patients to step beyond their habitual limitations—and begin to see their "incurable" conditions as curable. Since I have been trained traditionally as both a nurse and a chiropractor, I was surprised when my desire to help patients uncover the root cause of their disease and actually heal themselves led me into the realm of energetic healing. The term *energetic healing* may seem unfamiliar to many of us, but it's just a modern name for a very old process—the process of connecting with the true self within.

How did I first discover that this simple process can lead to radical shifts in healing? In my own life, one significant memory—of connecting with my true self—stands out from all the others. An innocent impulse, "I want to go to Europe after graduation," led me into a whole new world. I don't know where that impulse came from. When I was still in high school, my family suddenly moved from a small town in Iowa to the metropolis of Galveston, Texas. In Iowa, my music teacher had praised and nurtured my talent for music. That meant a lot to a kid who came from a family that was poor not only financially—but poor in feeding my spirit.

Maybe I gained enough confidence from my music teacher in Iowa to foster a thought that no member of my family had ever considered possible before. Maybe just stepping outside of all the small, little movements in life (like when we moved to Galveston) started me thinking a little bigger. I remember thinking, *This is really nice just to up and go somewhere new—this is something I can do.* So in that moment I decided, *When I graduate. I want to go to Europe.*

The next thing I remember is walking into a travel agency one Saturday afternoon and saying, "I'm planning a trip to Europe, and I need some information." I had no plans, no ideas, and no thoughts in mind, nothing. I just started discussing the idea with the agent, and it became more and more possible as we talked. The agent and I finished up my travel plans, and that was the first experience in my life where I was stepping into something bigger than I'd ever been in before.

What I notice, when I look back on this experience, is how *subtle* these signposts are in our lives. These subtle signposts, these things that just show up, mark the point in time when we decide to step into a new experience that is completely foreign to us—*or we decide not to*—and that decision is life altering.

I look for these signposts when I am working with patients. I see these signposts as points of leverage—as gaps in the continuity of our habit-driven lives where we all have an opportunity to make a shift—or not. If my patients can leverage these openings, access new opportunities for growth, and step out into something completely foreign (to the previous experience they have had in the safety of my office), they can shift.

My patients have been eager to share their stories of healing, and I felt that the subtle, underlying mechanics of healing would reveal themselves most clearly through their actual experiences. Healing is a process. And the steps of healing that one can identify through these stories reveal themselves as universal principles that can be applied in any medical practice.

How does all this relate to medical intimacy? In our rush toward efficiency and our worship of the bottom line, modern medicine does not have time for medical intimacy. Yet the depth of communication necessary for healing our relationships with our family and friends, our work, and most important, our relationship with ourselves and even the very cells of our bodies *requires* that we cultivate the most refined levels of intimacy. Intimate awareness of ourselves is the first and most basic step of healing. And the next steps of healing are accessible only after we have achieved this working basis of intimacy—both with ourselves and with others.

So this is the purpose of this book: to uncover these delicate steps of true healing, as illustrated in the lives of my patients and in my practice. Not surprisingly, these are the same basic steps we can all use to create for ourselves a life of abundant well-being.

CHAPTER 1

Curing the Incurable: The Basics of Medical Intimacy

One day about twelve years ago, Sam walked into my treatment room desperately seeking help. Sam suffered from trigeminal neuralgia—extreme nerve pain in his face. He had been referred to me by one of the best neurologists in the area. The neurologist had tried everything he could think of to eliminate the pain, including surgery, but nothing had worked. Having heard local reports of my unique approach to health care and my success with difficult cases, the neurologist had started to wonder, *What could this guy, Coram, do for my patients?* So he sent Sam to me.

This man was in horrible agony when he walked into my office. His facial pain was like sticking a hot poker in his cheek and leaving it there all the time. The memory of it still makes me cringe. Of course he was taking antidepressants and pain medications because the pain had gone on for six years.

I told Sam, "It's not going to do any good if I do things that other people have already done for you—things that haven't helped."

So I started exploring with Sam other aspects of his life. We talked about his work, his family, his recreation, and whatever else came to mind. "This is going to seem crazy," I told him, "but is there anything you have ever done that made the pain worse, or better—anything that changed the sensation?"

"Oh yeah," answered Sam, "but I told my doctors about that years ago, and nobody believed me or paid any attention to it."

Wow, I thought, *that's a neon sign right there.* "So what is it?" I asked him.

"Well, I have a rowing machine at home," said Sam, "and when I'm doing the exercise, my face seems to feel better. But the doctors didn't seem to be interested. They said I was using the muscles of my arms, not my face ..."

Immediately I asked Sam to take his shirt off. "I want you to reach for the ceiling," I told him, "while I take a look at the muscles in your back."

Sam lifted his arms up, and the scapula on the side of the pain didn't move. Normally, when a person lifts his arm up, the whole scapula moves up with it. You can't extend your shoulder completely without the scapula moving.

Sam proceeded to tell me that he had worked for twenty years at John Deere. He worked on a line, and his job every day was to repeatedly pull a lever with that arm. What happens with any repetitive stress injury is that we get micro-tears, and cumulatively over the years we get micro-scars. I concluded that over time the micro-scars had probably glued his scapula in place.

"Let me see what I can do with that stuck scapula," I told Sam.

At least I knew it was in the neighborhood of the facial pain and therefore worth addressing. So I worked at getting under the scapula with my hands. That's all I did. It was painful, but he was a tough guy, so I was able to free up his scapula in only two visits. After that, his facial pain was gone. That was when

I first started discovering soft-tissue issues that no one else had been addressing.

What did I add to the mix that allowed Sam to finally get rid of his almost unbearable facial pain? How did I, in a small town in Iowa, get a reputation for helping to cure the incurables? First, very simply, *I actually listen to what these patients say.*

The power of *listening*—the patient knows what he or she needs if we will just listen. Over and over again, I have seen in my practice that the patient knows what is wrong, and *he or she knows with some innate inner awareness what to do about it.*

If we are willing to just sit there, to honestly listen and be open to them, patients will express what their needs are and how to fulfill them. They won't use the complicated clinical words—that's for the doctors to figure out. A doctor can't demand that a patient rise up to some high level of technical jargon before he or she will take the patient seriously. He or she can't take the attitude of, "You, lowly patient, come up here and communicate with me at this high technical level if you want me to do something to help you." The doctor is the person with the training. He or she needs to translate his or her technical knowledge into everyday language. Doctors need to talk to their patients just like any person talks to any other person and try to understand what they are saying. The worst thing they can do is just dismiss whatever the patient is trying to communicate.

So this is how I create that lovely feeling of relaxed intimacy that patients always feel in my office. They report often feeling as if they are talking with their best friend. And nothing can shake their sense of safety, so they can say anything.

When I use the term *medical intimacy*, I mean a relationship with the patient that is sensitive and attentive enough to allow the free flow of true communication, where the patient feels safe enough to speak freely and trusts the doctor enough to know that what she says is actually being heard. For true healing, this same quality of intimate communication must be developed within each patient. The patients must feel safe enough to listen to their own inner truth and free enough to communicate their inner truth to themselves and to others.

But building a sense of intimacy, either with oneself or with others, requires many elements. The first is listening with an open heart and an open mind. The second thing we must add is trust. That's what a lot of doctors don't do anymore. They don't trust. They don't trust their patients. And that encourages their patients not to trust themselves. If the patients stop trusting themselves, that impairs their healing process. They can't communicate with themselves intimately if they don't trust themselves. So if we are going to talk about intimacy, trust is a huge part of it—a huge part.

A lot of people show up at a doctor's office with problems, and the doctors don't believe them. "You're exaggerating," the doctor says. Or he or she dismisses the patient altogether with, "You're making more of it than it really is." I've even heard of local doctors telling their patients, "You think your back's hurting? I've got a lot of back pain myself!" In fact, doctors will even argue with their patients.

Many patients report that when they go into a doctor's office and the doctor doubts what they say to him, they either have to doubt themselves or doubt the doctor. Either way, they need to put some distance between themselves and that doctor. The sense of pulling away to protect oneself, that separation, is the opposite of intimacy. The relationship with that doctor at that point is no longer a creative one in which both parties are free to share their thoughts and feelings in an uncensored manner.

This is the opposite of what people are looking for when they are dealing with a health problem that doesn't have an obvious solution. When they look to a doctor for help, they are looking for an environment in which the doctor and the patient can discover new ideas together, possible solutions we're not already aware of. They need to broaden their awareness in the doctor's presence, not squash it.

We need to realize that many patients in the distress of sudden illness go to a specialist they have never met before. They are faced with a possible diagnosis, second opinions, quick life-altering decisions, and maybe surgery, all in the presence of people who are complete strangers. This is shocking, especially if there is not a sense of intimacy and connection felt with the doctors and nurses who are literally invading one's body—while also stimulating a huge range of delicate feelings. People who are ill feel vulnerable, overwhelmed, and often helpless. The big issues of life and death pop up in their faces. These are moments of extreme physical and emotional delicacy. Having a strange doctor the patient has never seen before cut into his or her body and crack jokes while he or she is operating inside the patient's tissues can feel it as a deep violation—like a rape.

I do realize that when I use the word *intimacy*, sexual intimacy comes to many people's minds. I chose intimacy, along with the implications, deliberately. I wanted to find a universal metaphor. Almost everyone understands the language of sexuality. Sexual experiences are compelling, deep, and basic to our very lives. Every one of us was born from a sexual act. If I describe our medical relationship problems metaphorically in sexual terms, everyone understands what I am talking about.

For example, doing surgery on a patient without the prerequisite foreplay—getting to know the patient, finding out his or her unique story, and addressing his or her very individual needs—is a violation, a rape. People can die in the process. Name tags get switched. Allergic reactions happen. Presumptions and lack of information lead to misdiagnoses, oversights, and infections. And worst of all, the patient's natural healing response, which is the only real healer, gets damaged or displaced.

I believe we need to go back to old effective medicine, where the family doctor treats generations of the same family and knows his or her patients well.

But more important is the quality of the relationship that a doctor or nurse has with his or her patients, no matter how long they have known each other. To be of any help at all, I must listen to my patients deeply enough to know what they need. Then I can draw on my expertise and be open to inspiration for a creative, out-of-the-box solution. Ultimately though, the most important relationship of all is my patient's relationship with himself or herself. When I foster a relationship of openness and intimacy in my treatment room, I lay the groundwork for my patients to discover within themselves the magic of their own healing. I allow them to become more intimate with themselves. That is the ultimate healing relationship.

CHAPTER 2

Giving Back Hope

Recently a patient named Sarah fell from the second-story loft of her new house and landed on a heavy wooden ladder. The ladder staircase leading to the loft had come loose while she was climbing up, and both Sarah and the ladder had crashed nine feet to the floor. Luckily no bones were broken, but her body was badly cut and bruised. Several weeks after the fall, her left leg was still extremely swollen with a huge dark bruise that was not fading. So she was referred to my office since I had worked with athletes in the past, and one of my areas of expertise is treating sports injuries.

In the month after her first visit, I noticed that Sarah began doing a lot of new and positive things in her life. She found a new weight-loss program that seemed doable and started following it. She began exercising regularly and lifting weights, and she attended to some paperwork she had been putting off. When Sarah mentioned these positive changes to me during one of her visits, I immediately replied, "Well, that's to be expected."

Why wasn't I surprised by these good shifts in Sarah's life but felt they were to be expected? Are they the result of some magical powers that I zap my patients with in order to create shifts for the better? Actually, it's simpler than that. I've found that the biggest miracle worker in improving a person's health is simply hope. When a patient becomes hopeful, I've come to expect to hear reports of all kinds of positive changes in their lives. Greater changes than I could even imagine. Let me explain.

The first time I saw Sarah, her leg was so bad. The natural tendency we all feel when we have a wound is to avoid touching it. We want to avoid doing anything with it and just wait it out. So people sometimes will be in this holding pattern. They might have a desire to do something to help themselves, but they hesitate to do it because they don't want to mess it up. So in Sarah's situation with that battered and swollen leg, I wanted to get a lot of changes going quickly. There were some concerns because as fluid sits, it starts destroying tissue, so you can get secondary problems. I really wanted to make a lot of changes in that leg right away. So as I was doing all that intense work, deeply massaging and manipulating her swollen, bruised leg, what came up for her was the realization, *Well, if he can do all of that without really hurting me, then maybe I can do some things I've been afraid of doing. Maybe my fears that I would hurt myself doing those things aren't valid.*

I talked to Sarah as I worked, even while I was intensely and vigorously working on her leg. "I know this hurts," I said. "I get that. But we need to make these changes right away." I told her, "When this fluid goes away, circulation and balance can be restored, and your leg can become normal again. I need to work all of that fluid out of there." She was able to trust me enough to handle that. She may not have made a conscious connection between my work on her leg and other possibilities for her life, but I think on some level she realized, *Gosh, I guess I'm not as fragile as I thought I was. Maybe I can start to do a lot more things!*

My work is about restoring hope. Clinicians ask me, "What

kind of homework do you give them?" But I don't like to give them a lot of homework because my homework would be too limiting.

I want my patients to go home and live their lives. And they'll go home and try something, and they'll see, *Oh, that doesn't bother me so much anymore*. And then they'll try something else ... And when they come back, they are doing ten times more than I could have made up for them to do the last time I saw them. "You're doing all that?" I ask in amazement. "Great, that's good."

So I help my patients notice how amazing their progress actually is, and that what they now experience as their normal behavior would have been extraordinary a few weeks ago. Wow, that's a solid basis for hope—hope that real healing is possible and that real healing is actually happening. There's no mysticism here, just simple caring.

That is what I want other clinicians to understand, that it is a human thing I do, not a special thing. And we need a lot of other clinicians out there to create a revival of hope. My intention is to bring all this back to a spiritual level. Let's bring out our finer selves, our inner angels. Let's bring out all the sensitivity, the resourcefulness, the great reservoirs of kindness and compassion that brought us into the field of healing in the first place. Let's awaken that angel within all of us so we can better serve and care.

We've heard about this problem in medicine for years, and I've written about it again and again in the papers—that doctors take away hope. They take the hope away.

All I end up doing with many people is just giving them back the hope they have been looking for, the hope they really want to give to themselves, the hope they have been nearly convinced is unrealistic, pie-in-the-sky, unsupportable. I help them prove otherwise. I help them notice, through their own experience, the indisputable evidence that their hope is realistic. They are improving. They can get better.

"Here it is," I say to them. "Yes, here it is. Hope." I just give them back their own hope. And when I do, they find the healer within themselves. I just set up the necessary conditions and get out of the way so they can continue with their own very personal healing process.

This nurturing of hope needs to spread beyond the doctor-patient relationship to all the relationships in a patient's life—family, friends, workplace, church, school, community—and most importantly, to his relationship with his inner self.

Notes from a Wider Perspective

I am frequently asked this question: "Is emotional healing *always* a precursor to physical healing?" The answer is no, not always. There are, in some cases, physical conditions that are just physical conditions. For example, when I work with athletes, they often sprain their ankle. Usually there is no emotional precursor to that injury. Unfortunately, I have seen in the nontraditional medical world a common tendency to assume that *everything*, whether it is an injury or an illness, is an emotionally based issue. This is not always true. If we don't heal the physical wound when it occurs (and this happens with athletes), it *will* become an emotional problem as well as a physical problem. The emotional baggage will tie itself into the physical condition and block fixing that physical condition.

I don't limit myself to using just one approach to healing when working with my patients—for example using *only* spiritual work, or *only* emotionally based work, or *only* physical work. What I have found in some of these difficult, complex cases is that patients weren't getting results because there were parts of their being that weren't being addressed. Physical conditions, if they are *only* physical conditions, can be treated successfully with physical treatments alone. That's true. But the longer we hold onto a physical condition, the more it permeates the being, which then can affect the emotional and the spiritual part of the person, and then we need to use more than just one approach to healing for it to be successful.

CHAPTER 3

Edges—A Space Where Miracles Are Born

Let's talk about edges.

When Kelly first entered my office, she was wearing a shoulder brace and was in a lot of pain. She had just broken her collarbone in a bicycle accident. She was sixty-two years old and had her first major broken bone. Her husband was disabled. She was immobilized. The bone had been healing very slowly, and her shoulder was frozen. The orthopedist had already informed her that she would be disfigured. The physical therapist had told her, "If you can reach up to a cupboard at a little above eye level, that's good enough. That's the best range of motion you can expect after such a serious break." I explained to her that I could start working with her as soon as the knitting of the bone had stabilized.

Kelly returned to my office three months later and began a series of treatments. After the initial bone trauma pain subsided, we began to work on extending the range of motion in her frozen shoulder. We started to explore the edges of her restriction.

While Kelly relaxed on the treatment table, I stretched her arm again and again to the edge of her pain, each time stretching her frozen shoulder a little further into what seemed to be a rigid wall of pain. She would moan, but they were good moans. I told Kelly that there was still a shoulder in there, but it had forgotten that it was a shoulder. Our job was to remind the shoulder of its function, its range. I would go deep and then deeper and deeper into the frozen muscles in her back to let them know that they were still alive. The muscles began to breathe. More from the fear of stretching her rigid muscles than from pain, she would cry. Kelly remembered other times in her life when she had become frozen, rigid with pain.

During one of these releasing sessions, I explained to Kelly why taking her to the edge of her pain brings up so much fear:

We all have edges in our lives, places in our personal universes where our planet is flat and we don't want to go near the edge or we might fall off. If we ever fell off that edge, we don't know what lurking annihilation might be waiting for us. The strange thing is that it is precisely when we fall off the edge of our world into the scary unknown—into the empty spaces between what we believe to be true and what we don't know to be possible—that we locate the magic.

This uncharted space, this undefined void, this space between and underlying the things we see as normal, is what scientists are now calling the quantum field, the seat of all possibilities. Physicists describe the quantum field as a field of pure potentiality. Potentially anything can happen there. It hasn't happened yet; we are waiting to see what it will be, but it could be anything—*anything*. Potentially in the next moment you could increase your range of motion by six inches, or you could give the whole process up and walk out of this room, or you could laugh, or you could see the solution to your biggest problem and walk right through it with ease. Anything can happen—and it always does.

So what does all this have to do with healing? When we want to heal, we often want a healing miracle. Miracles are simply events that we observe that don't fit our beliefs of how the world naturally functions. But miracles happen every day. The miracle of birth is still way beyond our understanding. The miracle of gravity is still a mystery. The miracle of you choosing to lie in my treatment room right now, at this moment, is unfathomable. What forces of nature came together at this very moment to perfectly arrange this one specific event?

Falling off the edge of your world into the scary and wonderful uncharted space, the void, the unknown, is a sure way to connect with the field of all possibilities where miracles are born. In the space where anything can happen, miracles can happen. I am here to gently support you to explore your edge—to invite you to step into the freedom of feeling anything is possible and to help you discover the tools you need to heal yourself.

Kelly's shoulder is normal now. She can stretch her arm above her head in the yoga child's pose without pain. She is not disfigured. Kelly is now sixty-three.

Why was Kelly able to trust me enough to allow me to take her beyond the edge of her pain? Her answer was simple:

"I felt safe because we were communicating honestly with each other. We were uncommonly open with our feelings and therefore secure in our boundaries. We had created a relationship intimate enough to feel respect and freedom at the same time. I respected Dr. Coram enough to trust his drastic manipulations of my shoulder. At the same time, I trusted that he was listening intimately enough to my body that he would stop whenever I needed him to. My sense of safety was created through medical intimacy."

Another example of how openness to the possibility of healing allowed a patient to explore the edge of a physical limitation:

The father of one of my regular patients had lost his sense of smell, and I was able to help him get it back. Of course this was only possible because I had already established the necessary relationship of mutual trust and respect that we are calling medical intimacy with his son, Jim. Jim was so enthusiastic about his own progress as one of my patients that he was certain I could help his father. So when his father came from Michigan for a visit, Jim made an appointment for him to see me.

His father was a university professor in the field of economics, and he had fallen on ice the winter before and hit his head. The injury had destroyed his sense of smell. The doctors at the Mayo Clinic told him that either he would regain his sense of smell in three months, or he would never regain it. His son told him that he thought I could help him even though a year had passed since the accident. His father came to me for two visits, we went through the healing process that I will describe at the end of this chapter, and he regained 50 percent of his sense of smell. This esteemed professor felt that 50 percent was good enough, and he was thrilled with any results at all.

I wonder what would have happened if he had wanted a full 100 percent recovery? What if we had deepened the sense of intimacy in our medical relationship so that we could have pushed the edges even further?

In both of these examples—Kelly's shoulder and the professor's sense of smell—the Western medical professionals had said the condition could no longer be reversed, that the body was a machine that was broken and could not be fixed.

But the body is not a machine. It is a living system, and living systems heal themselves. Good doctors know that all they need to do is set up the conditions so healing can take place. Setting up the conditions for healing is the active expression of a person's intention to create better health for themselves. With the impetus of the right intention, the body will heal itself.

I saw Kelly's shoulder as a whole working shoulder and moved her through the rigid edge of her pain. When Kelly thought the shoulder would break if I moved it farther, I assured her that the shoulder would be fine. When she sobbed with grief and pain, I comforted her. When Kelly feared the predictions that her shoulder would never completely heal would come true, I replaced her negative images with a vision of a whole shoulder that knew how to move like a shoulder. I helped Kelly believe that she could heal.

The professor with the head injury for some reason believed his son when he said that I could help him with his "incurable" loss of smell. When his sense of smell started to return, he was overcome with the contrast between never smelling again, which also meant never tasting again, and smelling and tasting at 50 percent. He felt the miracle was good enough as it was.

The point of these examples is that it is from the intention to heal, which can only be based on an honest belief that we actually can heal, that healing is possible. The intention to heal and the underlying belief in the possibility of healing allow us to explore the edges of our doubts and create the conditions for miracles to happen. And in order for us to feel safe enough to test that intention, to step off the edge of our known world into the radically unknown realm of healing, we also need to create a relationship that is intimately honest and open enough to support our taking that risk. And we can create this relationship in the safe context of what this book is now defining as medical intimacy.

Notes from a Wider Perspective

In describing the work I do with patients in my office, I talk a lot about depth and connection. So what exactly do I do in these sessions? And what are the steps I use to get to a level of depth and connection with my patients that allows for healing that is transformational in nature?

What I have noticed is that every time I go into a deeper place with someone—for just a moment—I feel like I can't breathe. The reason this happens (my breath suspended and struggling to find its own rhythm) is that I am matching the breathing pattern of the patient. I have to take my breath, in that moment, out of its own rhythm to match their breath.

(Why does this happen? In order to create the sense of trust and safety necessary for this deep level of healing, the patients have to believe ... *that I am them*.)

So the first step is that my breathing pattern changes. Next, there is a temperature shift that I feel—where I am becoming *more* aligned with their physiology. And finally, there is a sense of dropping into—as if I jumped out of a plane, and I just kind of fall into this resonant space. Once I am in that state of resonance, a thought will arise: *What's in this space?* I can look around. Only my own thoughts are there, but it's almost like having a dialogue. I can ask questions. Not verbally of course; it's not like I am speaking something that anyone could hear, but internally I go through a dialogue of asking questions. And then I'll be presented with visuals. Sometime there are answers that come. Sometimes people show up. Once I'm in that space, then whatever is in that space, I get to see.

How do I get into that healing space? Only by giving that person *a sense that I am them.*

When I help couples do some of this work, I teach them that they each have to be in the genuine space of being there *for the other partner.* If there is any sense from one or the other of the partners that "I am here *to take* from you," from that moment on, we're out, and we are done with the whole process. They can no longer settle into a depth that can allow for true transformational healing. My hand might still be on one of them to support them in the process, but the session is over. So deep healing is only achieved by creating that space of safety where both partners feel: "I am truly there for *you.*"

Sometimes, when working with a patient, I don't get a complete drop in to that space. I get in a little bit, and then I stay at that partial level for a while, wherever that level is. This hesitation, this holding back is just the person's inner self trying to evaluate, *Is this threatening? I've let them get closer than I've let anyone get in a while, so I want to see—why are they here?* When I teach this process to others, I say, "Just hold that space, just stay there. Don't force. Don't leave. Don't become too demanding."

When I talked earlier about creating a dialogue in this space, if I ask a question at that time and I don't get an answer—I just wait. Then I might pose another question—and then again I wait. Don't barrage that delicate space with a lot of inquiry right away, because once you're in and that connection has occurred, the person is going to share whatever he needs to share with you. You don't have to do much. The "much" work is getting in. That's the work, getting into that space. Once you're in, he is going to tell you what is wrong, and he is going to tell you how to fix it. Be quiet. The work is getting in.

CHAPTER 4

Setting Our Intentions: Consciously Examining the Role of Intention in Healing

An ancient East Indian story tells of a wife who saved her husband from Yama, the god of death. It seems that Yama came to collect her husband one day to fulfill an earlier prophecy, and the wife, fearless in the face of impending death, followed her husband as the god of death carried him deeper and deeper into the underworld. The wife stubbornly stuck by the side of her husband despite all the trials that Yama inflicted to try to make her give up. Finally, out of utter respect for her steadfast courage, Yama let both the husband and wife return to the land of the living.

Kelly felt this was the story she was living when she first brought her husband to see me. She was facing the seemingly impossible challenge of trying to help her husband turn around a chronic disease, a disease that the medical establishment has always considered incurable: Parkinson's disease. Her mother, a former nurse, had died a few years before from the side effects of Parkinson's medications. The ruts of "inevitable outcomes" were deeply carved into the underlying groundwork of what Kelly believed to be true about the disease. She wanted to change her beliefs of what was possible. But she needed concrete, personal, real-in-the-moment examples to smash through the walls of modern medicine's expectations that healing, for her husband, was impossible.

Months later during one of her own therapy sessions, while I manipulated her back muscles to help her to release some of the rigidity in her spine, she asked me to give her examples of how intentions could actually translate into concrete results. Kelly wanted to believe deeply enough that she and her husband could, in truth, set the intention for him to get well—based on a belief that it was actually possible—and then act on it as real. Real intentions for real healing, not just palliative therapy. And she wanted her husband to believe it as well.

Kelly had already experienced healing in her own body (through our work together) that was beyond what her doctors and therapists had thought to be possible. We had broken through boundaries together that she had been told were *real*. She knew that dissolving the boundaries of dis-ease was a frequent outcome for patients in my practice. Now she wanted me to help her believe that she and her husband could do the same thing.

All this believing. It sounds like an old-fashioned Christian revival. But people are actually, truly healed at some Christian revivals. And opening up to the possibility of believing we can heal, even in the face of a seemingly incurable situation, obviously worked for those people.

There is a common belief about belief—embedded in many approaches to healing—that our beliefs determine our experience. From this it follows that, if we can only change our beliefs, our reality will change. Although this is true on one level, it is not the nitty-gritty work-a-day level where most of us live our daily lives. And the way this insight is often applied can actually be quite destructive to healing.

If I read in a book, or I am advised by a well-meaning friend that my illness is caused by my false beliefs, and that all I need to do to heal is to change my underlying attitudes or beliefs—then if I do not manage to change enough to get rid of my illness and get well, I might feel that I have failed. My negative self-talk might be: *I created this situation in the first place. This is all my fault. So if I can't change my beliefs right away and turn this thing around, I deserve to suffer the consequences.*

This is a bad place to end up, being sick and then feeling like it's my fault on top of it.

As I see it, belief that actually initiates change, belief that heals, belief that causes transformation in a person's life, only occurs when the belief is experienced at the deepest level and connects the person with his soul. Soul language is a language of wholeness. It unifies the whole person. A belief known to be true by the soul goes all the way through the person, creating shifts in the heart, mind, body, and even the environment. I call this kind of healing *transformational.*

Changing our beliefs on the surface level is just mood making. It might uplift us temporarily, but when the superficial effect of the mood making wears off, and we see that nothing has magically healed or changed for the better, we find ourselves more discouraged and doubtful than before. We might feel betrayed, or deluded, or powerless. Or we might feel that we have failed. Either way, the problem is not with the belief itself but from the depth at which we experience the belief to be true. And that depth of experience is based on the depth of our personal relationship with ourselves—as well as with our entire family, community, and culture. Changing beliefs is not a superficial process. In my experience with my patients, changing the beliefs that form the basis of our intention to heal is ultimately an organic, holistic transformation on the deepest level—the level of the soul.

Let's get back to Kelly. Kelly already had an awareness that her inner intentions were key to her healing and her husband's healing. She also knew that her underlying beliefs formed the foundation for any intention she might have. What she desperately wanted to understand was how to smash her doubts about healing. She wanted to "get it" so deeply in her bones and sinews and soul that her inner intention could actually transform her life—that her belief would become strong enough to extend to her husband as well and help them both heal.

So now let's talk more about intention and the relationship of our intentions to our beliefs.

Intention brings all of my patients to see me in the first place. They come to see me only because, for some reason, they think I can help them feel better. But nobody comes with the intention that they will get better right away, because they don't believe that it's possible. Take, for example, the athletes I work with. For years I have helped athletes with sports injuries get back to playing much more quickly than their coaches or parents or physicians ever thought possible. How do I do that? It's simple, really.

As I said before, the athletes don't come here intending to go back to playing their sport quickly. Their intention is just to get better, or to get rid of their pain, or to become more balanced overall. But once we work with the whole injury and get the athlete to a level where I can say to him, this is really better, this is good—then I can help him step into the next, more powerful level of belief and resulting intention. The athlete can feel the improvement—and I can verify the clinical extent of the improvement with my expertise. "You don't have to wait two weeks to go back into training," I can then suggest to the athlete. "You can go back right now. And the best way to find out if you are ready," I continue to assure him, "is to go do something. Test it. That's what we mean by being back. It means to just go do something. So go back to practice this evening."

"*Really?*" the athlete will ask.

And I tell him, "Sure!"

Parents and coaches and even the athletes themselves are shocked by how quickly I am able to help them get back into playing their sport. And it's the same for my patients with other health issues. I've observed this over and over again. When we start to feel better, that is the time to challenge ourselves to do something that we haven't been able to do for a while, something that we don't think we are capable of doing because we are sick or injured. "Now that you're closer to being healthy, reward yourself," I tell them. "Go and have that experience you've been putting off and see what happens!"

If they are successful—and they usually surprise me by doing more than I thought they were capable of doing—my patients realize that this is not just something the doctor said, some pie-in-the-sky daydream that they had just convinced themselves to be true. Instead they have just proved to themselves through their own chosen activity that they are on a new platform of functioning. The reality is that they can. There is realness to it because they did it.

My wife asked me last night, "How is it you can help some people and not others?" I told her that it goes back to the intention of the patient. The patients I work with have to believe in the *possibility* of getting what they want in their lives—because if they don't, if they are completely full of doubt, the doubts will block any intention that we might try to set in motion. I can't help those patients in any really significant way. It's impossible.

People have doubts come up in their minds all the time. I want to inspire them in the face of all their doubts. Does that mean there is no possibility for them to reverse their conditions because they have doubts? Not at all. Doubts are natural. I am talking about a deeper level of belief—beliefs that we hold so close and dear to our hearts that we find it more painful to question those beliefs than to continue our illnesses. These are the doubts that can block the flow of healing.

Doubts arise naturally when we are confronted by something that we don't believe to be true. Some underlying presumption of ours, conscious or unconscious, contradicts what we are hearing or seeing or feeling, so we feel doubt. Doubts can be a great tool for us because they are just a red flag telling us to look for the underlying beliefs that are bringing up the doubt.

Examining our doubts can help us locate unconscious beliefs that are blocking our way. But in my experience, actually challenging our underlying beliefs isn't easy. Kelly and her husband were willing to question their beliefs—to venture outside the box of modern medicine. They were willing to look for the root cause of Parkinson's disease in the realm of emotions, beliefs, and behavior as well as the physical levels of nutrition, microorganisms, and toxins. They searched Western, Eastern, and alternative medicine. They sought spiritual answers. They were highly motivated, because they were both trying to reverse a condition that modern medicine had defined as incurable. They couldn't rely on the conventional answers, because the conventional answers were no longer serving them. Kelly and her husband had been thrown out of the box of conventional thinking with no answers from Western medicine to support them.

You see, we all set up our own underlying foundation of beliefs that explain to us how the world works based on what we have been taught by our parents, our teachers, our trusted friends, and the community and media that surround us. If someone or something challenges that system of underlying beliefs, we naturally respond defensively. We've depended on that system of belief to run our lives safely for years. So our instinctive gut reactions start to run a defensive dialogue in our minds. It goes like this:

People I respect and honor have told me that this system is an honest system. How dare anyone question that? And furthermore, my parents (or my teachers or my friends) knew what they were talking about. How dare anyone tell me that my parents (or my teachers or my friends) were wrong? But then again, if something else is true and my parents (or my teachers or my friends) didn't know what they were talking about regarding this system—then how many other things that they told me might not be true? In fact, that makes me wonder altogether—what can I really believe to be true and whom can I really trust?

I've seen patients go into a tailspin when core beliefs like these begin to crumble. But it's a healthy tailspin, and it leads them toward finding for themselves a more useful set of beliefs.

Both Kelly and her husband have shifted a lot. I prefer to work with patients who are desperate to heal. Desperation shakes all these things up. When Western medicine clinicians tell you that you have an incurable disease or that you have only six months to live, you might think, *Screw my relationship with my parents, or my religious beliefs, or my boss. If I don't change something soon, I am going to die!*

An example comes to mind of a young man, a new patient of mine, who has cancer. He belongs to a very strict religious sect. He had a hard time feeling comfortable with the description I gave him recently of how I do my work due to his strict religious beliefs. So I thought to myself, *The next time I meet with him, I'll describe my approach to healing in a different way.*

I met with him this morning. I started talking with him about biblical principles. I used some biblical references to illustrate principles of healing and then suggested that we try some of the healing processes that are based on these biblical principles. Somehow, that different approach set him at ease—and he was able to allow the process of healing to unfold. I was really surprised. Possibly, because he has cancer, he is desperate enough to allow some of the restrictions of his belief systems around his religion to fall away. Whatever the reason, I am hopeful for his future.

If you are hurting enough or scared enough, you might be willing to risk jumping out of the box—even if that means risking making a mistake, or failing, or even hurting yourself. People have nothing to lose at that point, so why not? In addition, your intentions often become clearer when you are facing long-term pain or death.

Fortunately, in such a state of crisis, our intentions become clearer. It is because our desire to live becomes so much stronger. It is also the time when so many of these apparent miracles start to pop up for my patients—when I am working with patients who have run out of options and are up against a wall.

When there is strong, uncluttered desire—a clear intention—the obstacles will rise up to be attended to, step by step.

Intention is more than a one-step event—it's a process with many interwoven aspects. For example, I believe the patient's original desire to come into balance and to feel better is important in other ways as well, reaching way beyond the physical body of the patient and affecting his whole terrain, his whole community, and his whole environment. Intention serves as part of the magnet that starts pulling people and resources into his life that can be of assistance—by drawing into his awareness all kinds of people and events that can be helpful.

Our intention itself starts to draw forth its own support to gather around that purity of intention. My patients come to feel a quiet intention within themselves to have this particular experience—tasting, touching, smelling, hearing or seeing internally, in their mind's eye—that specific experience as a concrete, in-the-moment event. Then all of a sudden, seemingly automatically, the possibility of having that experience becomes greater.

So I tell my patients, "Offer up your desire, offer up your intention, and then allow God and his universe to respond."

Any injury or illness can be seen as simply the body being out of balance. So the first question we need to ask ourselves is, "How does the balance of the body relate to the overall system we are living within?" And the next question is, "What do we mean by the word system?" All the multiple influences that affect the health of our bodies—mental, emotional, physical, spiritual, environmental, and cosmic—must be taken into account when we are considering the health of the very complex system we are calling the human being. They must be taken into account because they all affect our state of health. Directly. Concretely. Whether we are aware if it or not. So by the word *system* we mean our entire personal world, inner and outer. And this entire system will naturally seek to keep itself in balance.

An illness may actually serve the overall system to help it

maintain some sense of balance. The words cancer, or Parkinson's disease, or MS don't mean anything at all to our overall system. They are just mental concepts—human words pointing to different flavors of imbalance of our bodies. Our system will strive to maintain the illness as long as the illness serves to help keep our system in overall balance. That is why we have to look beyond the illness if we want to effect a cure.

Illness is a symptom of imbalance in our body, but based on the many successful turnarounds that I have witnessed in my patients, I see that the illnesses and even injuries are often used by our larger systems as a tool to create more balance overall.

The disease is, in effect, the big overall system's way of helping itself survive and keep itself in balance. That disease is some sort of friend to our system rather than the enemy. That's a hard concept to grasp. We are used to seeing disease as the enemy to be conquered.

I understand the difficulty with this idea. The first step in understanding how this balancing process works is to recognize that we all have needs essential to the survival of our overall systems. If we discover new ways to fulfill those needs, we often see the distress of our current injuries or illnesses simply fade away. The system no longer needs the disease or injury because the balance can now be maintained in a much healthier way.

We've defined our illnesses with words derived from our limited ideas of what we think that illness is—from what we think is happening. But when we truly realize that our particular imbalance is tied into a bigger system, that we need to find bigger solutions to our dilemma, then we can address the imbalances in a much more direct way.

These are big thoughts. I am saying that the most direct way to heal is through addressing the big picture, the really big picture, which includes our families, our spirits, our God, and our whole personal world—as well as just our bodies. And it is as simple as saying—and I'm saying this to God, "Thy will be done—whatever Thy will is," without saying that I want to live, or I want get rid of this cancer, or this Parkinson's disease, or this MS or this whatever.

Let me give you a simple example that I've seen repeatedly in my practice. Many times, when a person develops cancer, they are showered with attention and love from their family and friends. All this attention and love is a very healing experience for the person with cancer. But what happens to the overall balance of the system when the treatments are over and all that loving attention disappears?

Unfortunately, if the person hasn't resolved the root cause of the cancer, his cure may not be permanent. The cancer symptoms often return.

But let me share with you quite a different story of another patient. One afternoon I walked into my reception room, and sitting on the couch looking directly at me sat the most beautiful woman I have ever seen. And I mean ever—flat-out gorgeous. I was stunned. *What is she doing sitting here?* was the first thought that flashed through my mind. It turns out that this woman had heard of my work from a friend and had driven the length of two states to see me. She had a form of cancer that kept returning after each apparently successful medical treatment. Her cancer test numbers rose and fell dramatically with no explanation. She told me right off that she came here because she had an inner feeling that I could help her.

Over the next few months as I worked with her, she became more and more relaxed and able to trust. She became more comfortable with her body, and her own inner stories began to naturally unfold to her. During one session, she spontaneously turned to me and said, "I've never before this moment told anyone in my life about this ..." And then she began to weep as she told her story.

(Of course, the very personal details of her story remain private and safe within the sacred confidentiality of the doctor-patient relationship.)

As the pain, the fear, the sadness, and the overwhelming experience of feeling powerless that had been stored and hidden in her body for years gently rose to the surface of her awareness, the story loosened its grip on her. Her behavior started to change. Over the next few months of treatment, she continued to release and let go. Gradually, quietly, without any great fanfare during that period, her behavior just naturally adjusted and changed. And with that change, the balance of her whole life system changed, and she is now cancer-free.

In her situation at the time she first came to see me, if our original focus had been to overcome the cancer, then what we would have tried to do was to remove the tool that was *guiding her in her life*—a tool that was necessary, at that point, to the overall balance of her system. We would have been fighting to remove something that didn't want to leave.

But by holding the simple intention of creating more balance and well-being in her life as a whole, we allowed the natural wisdom of her body to guide the process of healing. In that space of surrender to the will of nature, we can begin to feel the subtle presence of obstacles—resistance to the natural flow toward balance. As our system begins its own process of seeking balance, we can start to feel that process as a flow. We can also feel any resistance that begins to impede that flow. At that point, we can find out what is blocking the path. And then we can begin to ask the question "Why? What is in the way of that?" So as we try to get close to that balance, the body will, of its own accord, reveal to us naturally, simply, and spontaneously what is in the way.

I can feel that flow and the obstructions to that flow in my hands. I feel it in the room. Or in the voice. Or in the story. Or in the symptoms of the patient. It is in any or all of those things put together and more. The clues arise in many different ways as long as we take the time to really listen and to really see. I have often felt that clinicians need to use their whole spectrum of senses in their practice, not just their passive senses (vision, hearing, touch). What distracts us when we look at a patient is that we use our passive senses. We just think to ourselves, *This is cancer* or MS or Parkinson's or simply a broken ankle. Using just our passive senses always gets us into trouble.

Any real story can shake apart the solidity of one's beliefs. If you can see in yourself a living example of intention *actually shifting your life*, then you might be able to let go of the boulder of fear you are holding in your gut. You might be able to trust that you can find your own path of healing as well.

I can give you an example from my own life of overcoming some pretty impressive obstacles on my way to becoming a doctor, starting with my own simple intention. But this would be an example of a life challenge, not a health challenge.

First you need to realize that my journey to where I am right now was not an easy one. I didn't grow up with any of the conventional advantages of a strong family, a good education, adequate social training, or a launching pad of financial stability. To put it in simple language, I grew up on the wrong side of the tracks. Therefore, the success of my intentions is all the more meaningful.

When I was just out of high school, I applied to the University of Northern Iowa. My grades put me right in the middle of my class. None of the numbers fit, so the university said no to my application. A few months later after I had joined the marines, a woman friend of mine who was also a marine said to me, "You can do anything that you set your mind to." That's all she said to encourage me—and she said it only once—but I believed her. When I got out of the marines, I still wanted to go to the University of Northern Iowa. That was my intention. That's what I wanted to do. At that time, my family was living in Texas, and again, applying to become a student through the standard application process didn't seem to work for me. So I just said to my family, "I'm going to go to Cedar Falls, Iowa, this weekend, and I'm going to talk to the admissions director of the university."

I got on a plane that Friday, flew back to Iowa, rented a car, and went to the office of the director of admissions at the University of Northern Iowa. He wouldn't see me; I wasn't on his schedule. So I told his secretary the whole story. "I just flew in from Texas," I said. "You didn't even have an appointment?" she asked incredulously. "No," I replied simply. "But I'd really like to talk with him because I'd like to come to this college."

So I just sat there in his waiting room most of the afternoon, and finally, at the end of the day, his secretary said that I could go on in. As I walked through the door into his office, the director of admissions greeted me by saying, "Now tell me this story again ..."

He had my application. He had all the reasons they had used to not accept me, and yet he said, "Well, Charles, each year we accept a few people on what we call probationary status. These students don't meet our criteria, but we give them a chance. Based on your story, it really does sound like you want to come here. But I don't get it. You didn't have an appointment. It's Friday.

What would you have done if you had been unable to see me?" I said, "I'd probably have come back on Monday." Then he said, "Well, you don't have to come back. You're accepted. You're on probation, but you're accepted."

So often we think it has to be something complicated, that it takes a lot to break through all the obstacles and realize our intentions. But in many cases it's just acknowledging that we have a desire, offering up that desire, taking whatever action we can, and allowing the cosmic radar to respond. Sticking with our intention to fulfill that desire doesn't imply some rigidity based on the fear that the desire can't come true. Just the opposite. As I mentioned before, when we relax into a feeling of *Thy will be done—whatever that is*, we feel relaxed, because we are surrendering to the love within us that is the source of that particular desire to begin with.

Sometimes our intentions are so very specific that the outcome can be quite literal. For example, when I desired to be accepted as a student at the University of Northern Iowa, I got accepted as a student at the University of Northern Iowa. But then I was naturally faced with the next step—what comes next? I found that I needed new skills and new kinds of support. As a young man, the first in my family to go to college, I didn't have any idea what being in college and staying in college demanded of a student. I didn't know how to study or attend classes or balance my social life with my studies. So as it played out, I just plunged into the social life and enjoyed exploring my fraternity's leadership opportunities without really attending to my studies.

Unfortunately, my desire was to get into the school. Once I was in, I didn't have a lot of information and support behind me. I had no understanding of what college was like. My desire, my strong energy was to get into UNI. But I had no idea of how to stay, absolutely no idea. I didn't even know what I needed to learn in order to succeed with the next steps.

Fortunately, some people showed up in my life who gave me some crucial guidance and helped me believe in myself enough to step up and move forward into the next level of growth in my life. People who play this kind of role in our lives are like angels who come to us when we need them, angels who can help us with the knowledge of what our next intention needs to be, and then the next, and the next one after that, and so on. And gradually we begin to see more clearly the "why" behind our intentions. We need to get to that place where we start looking at our whole world as—not about getting this goal or that particular goal—but as seeing our whole life as a spiritual experience. This puts all the particular incidents in our life into a bigger perspective.

This book is just a story of people's actual experiences. And after we have told their stories, it comes down to this: do we believe that the stories are true? And then the next question: do the stories help us start to believe that whatever we want, whatever we thought might be a miracle beyond our reach, is possible? If we can get to that point, if we can hold that belief, that delicate knowing that *it is possible*—that will take us to the place where *anything can happen*. And it will. But in the absence of that, there is a limit. There's a limit. And then we're stuck with our old belief system.

Nobody likes the feeling of being stuck. That's why, when we find we can't move forward in our lives, we reach out to others for help. In fact, in my experience, I've found that there are angel-like helpers we draw into our lives to help us expand our belief systems and break through our inner limitations. Here's how it works.

If we're stuck within the limits of our belief system, even the desire and intention to look outside that system for answers can soften those limitations. Then we find people who have a broader vision, greater experience, and more knowledge in the area that we want to expand into. We call for our angels. But the problem is, when they come into our lives, do we believe that they can help us?

It's kind of like having an angel standing in front of us and saying to us, "You've asked me to come into your life. Now you have in front of you what you've been asking for." So it's up to us to step into this new partnership like we're receiving a gift that we've already been wanting. We just need to step into it. To accept it. To use it.

The people who can help us, like angel guides, show up in our lives because we are the magnets. We bring them in. But then we think, *Hmmm. Am I worthy of this in my life? Do I trust it?* We have to learn to believe that what we ask for shows up. It's coming. It's what we've asked for. So now receive it. Accept it. Allow it.

And that's when it shifts, at that very moment.

CHAPTER 5

Dissolving Self-Destructive Patterns—Shifting Attention to the Health of the Whole System

I do not see any of my patients as people who are sick. When I look at each patient, I see a perfectly well and vital being who has temporarily forgotten who he or she is. The patient usually comes in because of pain or major distress in the body. But I do not focus my attention on the illness.

When a new patient comes into my office complaining of some discomfort or even some major illness, I usually see in front of me a healthy and whole person is who hosting a self-destructive pattern. This self-destructive patterning usually begins its development during an experience of extreme overload to the system—often in early childhood.

Some negative or positive experience was just too much for the body to handle at that time. For example, a toddler with fighting parents might have felt he would be hit or even die if he made a noise while his parents were fighting. So that child develops a pattern, such as withdrawing or clamming up in situations where a person close to him is angry. And maybe the danger was real or the response of withdrawing was necessary when the toddler started using it to cope. But when he has become an adult, it is clearly not true that he will die if he makes a noise while someone is fighting. And yet the old fear or withdrawal pattern persists.

This particular stress response, along with innumerable other stress responses, gets repeated and gathers reinforcements until the body becomes more and more imbalanced through perpetuating this self-defensive pattern. The response pattern is no longer needed, but the body forgets how to work without it.

A patient complained to me about her chronic eating disorder. Whenever she tried to lose weight, she would actually end up gaining weight. And her weight was killing her. The pattern I saw was a mechanism of stuffing her feelings. Whenever she would start to have one of these knee-jerk, totally automatic responses to the current events in her life based on these unconscious feelings stored in her body from past injuries (emotional or physical), she would snuff out the feelings with food. Usually unhealthful food. Why? The feelings coming up demanded that she take action. But feeling those feelings and taking appropriate actions to deal with the actual situations would have broken her pattern of using food to avoid the feelings. And she had used that pattern to keep herself safe for most of her life. She trusted the pattern to work for her as if her life depended on it. So she compulsively ate food, any food, whenever the pattern demanded that she block her uncomfortable feelings.

These patterns get repeated so frequently with many people that they seem to take on a life of their own. Often, the self-destructive patterns' resistance to change is so powerful that it's as if they are fighting for their own survival. Everything hates to die—even our unconscious, outdated behavior patterns.

I use this example to illustrate how I look at the sickness in our bodies. I see our illnesses as unconscious self-defensive survival patterns—patterns of behavior that override the natural responses of the body and throw the whole system out of balance—patterns that get repeated frequently enough to take on a life of their own. These patterns want to feed themselves in order to survive and grow, and all of our patterns grow through repetition.

The body repeats these patterns because circumstances pop up in one's life resembling the initial trauma or event. The second and third and fourth and one hundredth time a similar event pops up, the body thinks it has to defend itself—and it responds automatically, without thinking, in the same way it responded to the original event. But the problem is that the responses gather momentum. They pile up on top of each other. Someone bumps into me, and I respond as if they have threatened my life. Ten percent of my response is appropriate, and 90 percent is piled-up momentum from the past.

That's why we call them triggered responses, like pulling the trigger of a gun when you only need a flyswatter. And until we neutralize the charge, we can't help ourselves. We just keep repeating the same increasingly loaded responses. Triggered feelings ... patterned response. Triggered feelings ... patterned response—repeated so frequently that the pattern will actually morph and change shape and do whatever it needs to do to survive. The only way to release the pattern is to embrace it without feeding it. Don't give it what it wants. Starve it. And then replace the pattern with a different reaction to the events of our lives that serves us better. But this must be done in a context of love.

How is this accomplished?

For my patients who are suffering from self-destructive behaviors and unwanted patterning, I create in my treatment room a space of love and simple acceptance, much stronger than the pattern itself. I encourage patients to surround themselves with a field of their own utter self-acceptance. Their own self-love. I help them locate self-love within themselves, and I also offer them the experience of my own total acceptance of who they are right now in that room. I use the process I described earlier at the end of chapter 3 to help give my patients a sense— *that I am them.*

With both of us securely cushioned by this space of love, I witness the self-destructive patterns demanding whatever they want. I just observe; I don't respond. Eventually I watch the pattern dissolve, leaving only an expanded field of love in the room. But this process takes strength, a lot of strength for both parties. The strength of discrimination and understanding. And the strength of patience and delicate attention. I must see clearly enough to differentiate between the patient's patterns, the patient's inner healthy state, and my own responses. Likewise, my patient must be willing to look honestly at her feelings and step out into the unknown territory of change.

Most health care practitioners don't have the time or sensitivity or patience to play such a demanding healing role. Also, many patients are expecting something or someone else to fix them, rather than taking charge of their own healing and exploring within. So there is great resistance to this type of therapy in standard Western medical practices.

But the rewards of this unusual approach to healing are great. The patients actually get well. Not just symptomatic relief. They change. They start focusing on what they want in their lives, now. Rather than returning again and again to what the pattern wants, the patient focuses more on what his larger, healthy self wants. To run, or swim, or play tennis, or ski. To love and be loved. To dance and sing with joy. To embrace success and the fulfillment of his desires. To make love. To be alive.

Notes from a Wider Perspective

My main job as a doctor and a healer is to help my patients open up to an intimate relationship with themselves that gives them the self-love and perspective to let go of their self-destructive behavior patterns. Self-destructive, I know, is a pretty strong word, and not everyone needs this kind of help. If a person was given all the love, support, and proper guidance he needed as a child and as a young adult, that person would probably never be drawn to my office for treatment.

But many people have personal histories with some degree of hidden pain and dysfunctional family patterning. They have learned hidden ways of dealing with pain—coping patterns that develop into various forms of self-destructive behavior. Repetition of these self-destructive habits over time creates the discomfort and dis-ease that bring hundreds of patients to my office for help.

Habitual, usually unconscious false beliefs (such as "I must not deserve anything better than this," or "I won't be able to handle the repercussions of standing up for myself," or "There's nothing I can really do to solve this") are definitely part of the self-perpetuating patterns of behavior that undermine our health. And these false beliefs can sabotage many of our most sincere intentions to change and to heal.

One common false belief is that if we ask God for something and we are meant to have it, then God will deliver it to us immediately in its fully manifested form. Like a fast-food drive-up restaurant. We just need to speak our order into the box, drive forward a few feet, and pick up our instantly prepared burger and fries. No fuss, no muss. No waiting. No discomfort or stretching or pain of any kind. No inner or outer work.

If the change we want doesn't come right away, we get discouraged and give up, falling back into the old familiar patterns.

There has to be action involved in healing—an openness to new ideas, a willingness to try new things, patience, and perseverance, all in a context of true self-acceptance and self-love.

When God and his universe answer our requests, we are usually given a road map—some intuition of a next step to take, an example of someone who has overcome a similar problem, some new opportunity coming our way, or some other clue from the environment. We are given the information of what we need to do to create what we have just asked for. The intention just starts the process and continues to direct this creative progress of healthy growth.

How do I as a practitioner redirect the patient's attention away from the seductive and familiar pull of old self-destructive patterns toward rediscovering the inner core of health within? What are the details? How does it work? The in-depth interviews of my patients in the following chapters bring to light six different personal accounts of this process. They all describe in their own words the experience of releasing some patterned responses to life that were harmful to their health and well-being. They also give us some detailed examples of the improved health and lifestyle these patients are enjoying as a result of this process of self-healing.

CHAPTER 6

Merging With Our Source— Expanding Our Perspective

Have you ever wanted to fix something that stopped working? I remember sitting down in the middle of my living room floor a few years ago and taking apart my Blu-ray player after it whirred and clicked off. I wanted to figure out what was wrong so I could fix it. The problem was that once I took it all apart and had all the pieces set out in a circle around me on the floor, I couldn't figure out how to put it back together again. It was so easy to take it apart—but I lacked the overall understanding of how the parts worked together, so it was impossible for me to reassemble all those levers and disks and washers and screws back into a working whole. I had to call and get instructions from the manufacturer.

The funny thing is—the same thing is true with our bodies. It is easy to mentally take them apart, to divide them into separate pieces like dermatology and dentistry and cardiology. But what about our understanding of how all the parts work together to make a whole? How often do we consult the original source about the blueprint that lies behind the movement of our individual parts?

The whole reason I am sharing these stories—the reason I asked patients to share the details of how they reversed their illnesses—is to help others find out how healing works. Poets say that "God is in the details." Perhaps these patients—through sharing the details of their own unique stories—can reveal to us what they consider to be the source of their unexpected healings.

The recurring questions I hear are: What is it about your approach to healing that allows patient after patient to reverse conditions that had stubbornly resisted healing before? How is it that so many of your patients find themselves curing their heretofore "incurable" conditions? And then recently, one patient asked me, "Might you be creating an environment that allows each patient, in their own way, to directly "merge with their source"?

Felicity is a patient who still comes to see me even though she lives many states away on the West Coast. Here is her interview, starting with the question, *what led her to seek the advice of a health care professional in the first place?*

"To give you an answer to that question that makes any sense at all," she said, "I'll first have to explain a little about my background. I grew up in a very tightly wound, highly emotional household. My father was a tortured soul—brilliant, alcoholic, and abusive. Both my parents come from very healthy (other than the mental illness and alcoholism), incredibly strong, sturdy DNA. So physically we don't have heart disease or cancer. It's the emotional element that gets us.

"It wasn't until I went away to college that I started to notice things in my life that weren't working well for me. I wasn't holding up well compared to the other students. I noticed that the others were moving comfortably through their days, through their classes, through their interactions with friends and colleagues.

In comparison, I was just so tightly wound. Just recently I had the realization, *Oh, this is what other people are calling anxiety.*

"The truth is, I have never really enjoyed myself while doing anything—I mean *anything*—but even back then I didn't know it. I just had this nebulous feeling that something was not right. I've been on a thirty-year journey trying to understand the mechanics of the knot inside me that I now call anxiety—attempting bit by bit to unravel within myself a tightly embedded, hard ball. The other students I observed at the time knew how to relax, how to play and have fun. They knew how to interact with each other. I would look at them easily joking with each other—playing with each other in a relaxed way—and I would wonder, *How do they do that? How do people think of things to say? How do they relax and have the courage to start joking and know it's going to work out without suffocating as I do with self-consciousness?*

"The result of all these nagging, fearful thoughts was that I ended up feeling incapacitated. Frozen. But I have grown to understand that this behavior is really the result of my response to childhood trauma. My pattern is to freeze—the result of living with some crazy energy from my father. My whole family behaves this way, including my mother and my siblings. I'm like a wild deer that has been chased by a cougar in the forest. *Maybe, if I am absolutely still and sort of disappear,* I think to myself, *the danger will pass me by.* I learned this behavior so well as a child that the pattern is embedded in the fabric of my being, and I don't know anything else. My family is from the West Coast, so we talk about it openly. The way we deal with stuff is with a lot of sarcasm. We jab, we laugh. And then, when we recognize the humor in our own patterns—we tend to open doors for others to share their experiences with us, as well.

"As a kid, I had horrible stomachaches from all the stress in my family—as did my siblings. Mother took us each to the doctor if it was acute enough. The doctors gave me Phenobarbital to relax my stomach. I also had terrible constipation. Everything would freeze. So then mother took me to a gastroenterologist who told me my problems were just from nerves and dehydration. The doctors had nothing to offer me as a cure. I didn't fit into any of their medical boxes.

"I don't do well with narrow conceptual boxes, like the current methodologies often used by the AMA and Western medicine. Let me explain why.

"A living organism has to be seen as a whole system. I'm not just a liver. I'm not just a heart. I'm not just a thyroid. Western medicine seems to break everything down into separate systems or boxes. Then these various specialists all run their tests. And yet nothing was showing up to explain my health problems through the tools of Western medicine. No one was going deep enough to uncover the emotional seed at the core of my condition.

"When I consult a doctor to help me heal some dis-ease in my body, what I want to know is—*what is at the basis of this uneasiness within me?* For example, if there seems to be a problem with my thyroid, then my question to my doctor is—What is upriver from my thyroid? What is downriver? And what is in the lake that feeds this river? Are there stagnant pools clogged with algae and debris? Is there an obstruction blocking the flow? Could there be an old dam in the way that no longer serves its original purpose? I am asking these questions because I am looking for the source of this problem with my thyroid—*within me*.

"I believe, from the basis of my own personal understanding of healing and of the body, that if I can release the inner source of my problem—if I can identify the source of the blockage upriver from, say, the thyroid—then presumably a normal flow can be restored. To me that means that I can then restore the unrestricted flow of health that is natural to my body—all the parts flowing freely, successfully communicating back and forth with each other and working together as a whole.

"I had a stressful job at the time I first went to see Dr. Coram. Everything around me in both my family situation and my work was very high stress. And finally it culminated when I was sitting in my office and *I realized I could barely breathe.* This was probably what people call a panic attack. I couldn't believe it was happening to me. I'm high strung, but I'm very highly functional. All of a sudden something wasn't working at all, and I was paralyzed. I couldn't do anything."

Felicity had first heard about me when her friend started coming to my office. Her friend told Felicity about our work, and Felicity knew right away that she wanted to make an appointment to see me. Felicity explained in her interview that since her husband was also a doctor, and a very good doctor, she was highly discriminating in selecting physicians for her own personal health care.

"I do a lot of due diligence before I even make an appointment.

"But when I go, for instance, to have my annual checkup and I see that the doctor I have hired to assist me isn't really listening to what I have to say—I'll just fire him on the spot. Maybe he is overworked, or he doesn't have the time or the willingness or the training, or maybe he is just too noisy in himself to settle down and listen to me with his ears, his mind, his heart, and his feeling level. Whatever the reasons, I think to myself, *What's the point? For others, this may work, but for me, it's just not working.* That's disease care, not health care.

"I get quite animated on this subject. Western medicine as we know it has become just another big business—and in my opinion, big business has nothing to do with healing. The sad thing is that many of the doctors have been forced to comply with this medicine-for-profit system. Most doctors don't seem to understand anymore how important it is to sit down, let the atmosphere in the room settle down into some quiet sense of receptivity, and then to just listen—to actually listen to what the patient might have to say.

"That's what medicine used to be. The doctor knew you, he knew your family, and he knew your home because he made house calls when you were too sick to come to his office. He knew the personalities behind the scenes because he was personally involved with the community he served. When a patient had a problem, he was able to listen to the story behind the words without the patient having to go into great detail. When I was a child, our family doctor was like that.

"Dr. Coram's ability to actively listen, in the way I have just described, was part of what first drew me to working with him. But even with both people listening, trust is not a given. Trust is earned in any relationship. And it takes time. With any relationship, it takes me a while to feel safe enough to open myself to actual healing.

"For example, when I first walked into Dr. Coram's office and saw him sitting behind the counter, we looked at each other, and my conscious reaction was immediate. *Yes*, I felt, *this is the right thing*. But the deeper parts of my unconscious mind take more time to feel safe. The only way I can describe it was that something beneath my conscious mind was not willing to allow any sort of interaction or communication. My distrust was so deep, the door was so closed, that even I was taken aback. So that took a while. I seemed to go through a melting process, like a melting glacier. It took a few appointments of treatment with

Dr. Coram before on both a conscious and an unconscious level I felt completely 100 percent comfortable with the process and his method of working.

"One reason this internal melting could take place is that Dr. Coram creates an environment with his work, a healing space that supports the process of healing. How would I describe it? It's not easy to put into words. It is such a subtle and abstract experience for me. Powerful but subtle. It reminds me of hearing a very high pitch. Something is so finely tuned in there, so highly calibrated, that it's like a tuning fork. When I'm in his office, I sense such a fine resonance that I feel like I'm being taken up within myself to a more refined, higher octave. How can I further describe it? Maybe if you can imagine yourself listening—like a musician in an orchestra sitting in a large, silent auditorium before a performance. Before the orchestra starts to play, the oboe tones a single note so that the entire orchestra can then tune itself to that same A note. All the different voices of the orchestra answer back with variations of the same note until a perfect resonance is created and they are all playing in harmony. The orchestra is playing in tune.

"It's just the environment that Dr. Coram creates. Something is very right there. I can feel it the moment I drive into his driveway. I still don't know what actually takes place in there, but I come out the other end of an appointment feeling settled and quiet—profoundly quiet and very whole. I find myself moving through my days after that with some new level of wholeness.

"I'm living on the West Coast now, so I don't see Dr. Coram as often. But each time I return to the Midwest for a visit with him, I am able to peel back more internal layers of healing within myself—and consequently in my relationships with others as well.

"All I know is that I become aware of more subtlety in my experience. As a result, I can choose to pay attention to those subtleties and start to understand, *Oh, here are the mechanics of what I am currently feeling.*

"For example, I may at that moment feel some pressure around my heart. In the clarity and subtlety of my awareness in that new wholeness, I can notice that it feels heavy, like pressure, and not problems with heart disease. That is an actual experience I had a few months ago. Here is how it unfolded.

"As I continued my visits with Dr. Coram, I grew to understand that this feeling or pressure I was noticing around my heart was actually fear—a shield of fear that I had gripped around my heart since childhood. Ever since I was a kid, I never wanted to get out of bed in the morning or meet the day. I dreaded getting up. I wasn't excited. When I saw Dr. Coram, I described this insight to him: 'I think the pressure around my heart is fear, Dr. Coram. Can we investigate?'

"Two hours later, I left the office, and I didn't think another thing about it. Months passed. A week or so ago, I asked myself, *What's different? Something feels different. That heaviness over my heart is gone! It's gone—just gone!* I keep testing within to see if I am feeling it again. But it is gone.

"If I tried to explain these personal experiences of healing to somebody like my mother or her friends, or even my friends, their eyes would glaze over. They might think I'm nuts or that I'm being taken for a ride, or any of the various suspicious things that one might think. But I've experienced it, and I know that my process of healing is real, beyond any question whatsoever.

"Of course again you might be wondering, how does all this work? I know that in the beginning, that was the big question in my mind. So to address that, let's go back to discussing just how

Dr. Coram creates this healing environment in his office. It starts, I feel, with his astounding willingness and ability to listen—not only with his ears or with his intellect but with his whole heart and with every fiber of his being. Not simply listening to what I say from the level or space of Dr. Charles Coram but from a place of standing in the River of Life, of being a channel between a higher healing power and myself. I speak to him from that place in me that is perfect and whole. And I also find the willingness to speak to him from that place in me that is blocked but willing and longing for wholeness. So it's between all those places that he's able to do what he does—from his intellect, from his heart, from his soul—from his willingness to give over and stand in that river and allow the whole dynamic to happen without having to make it wrong, or fix it, or impose anything restricting. It's between that willingness on his part and my willingness—to tap into my unconscious self, my higher power, and my bigger body of wholeness—that all this takes place.

"It's a journey of what can happen when willingness to give over to a higher healing power is there. Personally, I feel disease is embedded in the emotional body. Certainly it is for me and my family. To find a person who is willing to step out of the way and go to those deeply fine, finely calibrated places—it just takes an enormous amount of silence and an enormous amount of courage and faith and humility on his part. I don't know how he does it—to hold that space. I just feel lucky that he's willing to do it. And the gratitude I feel is beyond words.

"I think it takes a huge amount of courage to walk into that treatment room day in and day out and meet people on that level. And it takes vulnerability. Dr. Coram is so willing to be vulnerable—like naked-on-a-mountain-side-in-the-killing-cold-and-gale-force-winds kind of vulnerable—and that is what I call true courage. He's not going in there with anything other than himself, his silence, his heart, and his ability to listen on all levels. I have never, ever in my life experienced someone who is willing to be that exposed and that vulnerable.

"And it is his courage and his willingness to be vulnerable that invites me to step up and meet him when I can. That is, when my conscious, subconscious, and unconscious parts are willing and able to do that. But that takes time, because there are many carefully constructed internal doors, thresholds, and rooms between my ultimate vulnerability and my persona in the outside world—a lot of doors that I'm not even aware of—that have been shut down tightly along the way.

"However, healing is a partnership—and Dr. Coram is many miles ahead of me in his willingness to be vulnerable. But his complete vulnerability invites me, encourages me, to join him somewhere up the road whenever I can. And that's an unfolding dynamic; it's a process."

Let me break into Felicity's dialogue here and explain why both the qualities of courage and vulnerability are *essential* when I am creating a feeling of safety for my patients. Courage, in the first place, is just the courage to be completely open. In order for the person I am working with to be open, I have to go first. I need the courage to be completely open in my clinical relationship with them.

Now here's the rub—there is a common confusion about the qualities of both openness and vulnerability. People often think of complete openness as a position of vulnerability. And many consider vulnerability itself to be unsafe. However, in my opinion, vulnerability is the strongest position that we can take. Because when we are open and vulnerable, our vantage point is real. We can see. We can see all around us. We can see what is really there. When I teach my patients about openness, I tell them it's like having your eyes open. Is it safer to have your eyes open? Yes, of course it is—but it's very vulnerable. If I close my eyes, it's going to be harder to do damage to the eyes. But what would your life be like if you kept your eyes closed all the time? You wouldn't get your eyes poked, but what could you see? That *vulnerability* of each of us having our eyes open gives us greater experiences. We are stronger because the information that we have is so much more accurate. And that accurate information gives us the ability *to respond most appropriately to whatever we meet* in our current situation. If we keep our eyes closed—yes, we'll be safe. We'll stay closed, and nobody can hurt us. But then we will have no idea of what is going on around us. There's no awareness when we keep our eyes shut—none at all.

Now let's return to Felicity's story of healing through the process of becoming aware of her own inner experiences:

"Let's face it: most of us are survivors. We have everything so neatly stacked in our minds—like little boxes neatly organized, carefully stacked one on top of the other, so we can go out in comfort and *function* in the world. And if we pull out and examine one of those boxes that we have so carefully stacked—*what is going to crumble?* Will it all stay up, or will it completely crumble? And who's going to fix that? The question that first pops out in front of my awareness is—if I go on this journey in this room and in this appointment today, will I be able to walk out of here and go back to my family, my job, my community and still function? (I was still afraid that I would be hurt if I was open. So if I started to open up in my everyday life, I might just freeze—because all the old fears would overtake me, and I wouldn't be able to function.) That's a huge risk—because those are the kinds of levels that Dr. Coram has gone to with me. Helping me to un-stack some of my boxes while still supporting me by standing in a flowing river of safety and trust. That takes pure mastery and courage on his part.

"Now, after working with Dr. Coram off and on for the last few years, I no longer have any panic attacks. I am reacting differently to the stresses that naturally come up in my life.

"You know the old term, boiling a frog? I think the healing process that I have been going through is like un-boiling a frog. The frog doesn't notice the water is heating up around him until it's too late and he's cooked. But moving in the opposite direction of boiling a frog is like waking up from a deep sleep—a very deep, uncomfortable, sad, dysfunctional sleep. It's like one day I might notice, Wow, I can move that finger! I didn't know that finger was paralyzed—but look at that! It's moving, and it can do this and this and this. And now all my fingers are moving! And my wrist and my hand, and wow, look at what my elbow can do! So that's kind of what's happening.

"As I mentioned before, it feels like the melting of a glacier. But it's happening so slowly and organically. I think that is part of the healing process for me—the feeling of allowing, of melting. The word *allowance*, a kind of deep acceptance, is so important in healing, I think. And for me as an individual, I need the deep acceptance that I came from a dysfunctional background, that I chose unhealthy things in the past, and now need to give myself the allowance of innocence, the allowance for healing to take place without putting it under a microscope.

"And patience is a word that goes side by side with allowance. I need to have the patience to allow the imperfection or lack of balance to stay as long as it needs to, because it didn't get here overnight—and it's not necessarily going to go away overnight—and so I need to allow that to be okay and to allow healing to happen in its own way and in its own time.

"The experience described earlier of a shield of fear lifting from my heart seemed like a very significant step of growth. Today, I am not noticing so much the lack of fear around my heart, because what I am experiencing more than anything these days is a profoundly big fatigue. I've always felt fatigue. Since I was a child, I have been stuck in a fight-or-flight pattern, and how much adrenalin can you run in a lifetime without becoming tired and depleted? Also, I think this fatigue is from pushing so hard the last couple of years—two years of helping distressed family members—and on top of that, for about a year I helped with a friend who had been hit by a car while riding his bicycle. Five days a week, I helped with his care, and I became his financial and medical power of attorney for a year. Next, we moved back to the West Coast right before Christmas. So it's been a really concentrated two years! I am pretty pooped—and my day-to-day experience is just profound fatigue.

"But I no longer have the heaviness on my heart. So I think as the fatigue lifts, and as I allow for more play—really schedule some playtime into my weekends and allow for more quiet time in my life—that it will be interesting to see how things unfold without filtering my life through fear. What will the new filter be? A whole new me! That's not something I've ever experienced before. I've lived my whole life through fear. All my decisions have been filtered through fear. All my relationships have been filtered through fear. So right now, coming out of the fatigue, that's what I'm watching for.

"I will say that I am much more stable and unshakable since we've been back. Our living situation is a little precarious right now. We've been renting a house that has been for sale, and the sale of the house is closing next month. I have no idea if we're going to stay in the house or move, and I'm not worried about it—I'm not afraid. I am living much more in the moment. I'm just waiting to see how this pans out—to see if the new owners might want us to stay for a year. But I have no idea if they are going to raise the rent, maybe horrendously. And I still say that's okay. It will all work out just fine.

"Normally I would be very, very worried—and sort of gnashing about it—but I am not. I feel more like water flowing down a hillside. When a rock comes, I'll just flow around it, or over it, or I'll sit in the pool for a while.

"It's really a process of waking up to these realizations or understandings of, *Wow, that's different. What just changed?* But it's so subtle at the time. I think as the fear is lifting, there is less of a feeling that I have to do this or that. Rather than some big, dark parental forces commanding me do something, I'm having more of an internal discussion, like, *what do I want?* I've never asked myself that before. What do I want? How does that feel to me? And I am speaking up for myself more often. 'No, that doesn't work,' I might tell someone, or 'I'm going to need more time on that decision,' or I might just say, 'You go on ahead without me.' This is all new territory for me. And yet I am allowing it. It's happening very organically. It's not planned, and I'm just finding that those mechanics are unfolding more and more in my daily life."

My goal of writing this book is to share these kinds of experiences of healing with other physicians, and with the public at large, so that this experience of medical intimacy can be recognized as an extremely important factor in the transformation that we are all looking for when we go to a doctor or some other health care provider to ask for help. Openness to listening is a capacity that each individual naturally has. If patients and health care providers would just allow themselves the space and the time to open up to the simple act of deep listening and simple receptivity, we might all begin to discover that our medical outcomes improve.

CHAPTER 7

The Power of Trust—Another Referral

Felicity was so delighted with the results of her work with me that she made an appointment for her sixteen-year-old niece, Elizabeth. Elizabeth was suffering from bouts of anxiety and depression, and she had left her home on the West Coast to live with Felicity and her husband so they could try to help her resolve some of these anxious tendencies.

"Before I came to Iowa, I was obsessed with getting perfect grades and getting everything perfect. I'm homeschooled, and it was the first year of my homeschooling. If I got even one part of my assignment wrong, I would feel just awful. There was so much anxiety around my schoolwork, so much angst, that it snowballed into anxiety about everything in my life. I didn't want to go outside. I was so focused on getting everything right that I was afraid to do anything. It got to the point where it was looking like I might have to go into an inpatient program. But my family decided that wasn't the correct thing for me. The antidepressant and anti-anxiety medication I was taking did not react well with my body at all—and at the same time I was putting all this food into my body that I later discovered I was allergic to. My body is so incredibly sensitive; it was just flipping out. So the whole situation snowballed to the point that I just stayed in my room. I really did not want to go out of the house—period.

"Eventually, instead of doing an inpatient program, I did go to Iowa to live with my aunt. I started a wheat-, dairy-, and gluten-free diet—avoiding the foods I was allergic to and eating the foods that my body needed—and then I stopped being so afraid of going out of the house. I was fine with social things—but there was still that obsession with my schoolwork. I felt like I always needed to get more done and to pressure myself to be better and better. Though it appeared that I was fine, internally I was really very conflicted and not fine. There was, in fact, a war going on inside me—even though people looking at me from the outside might think that nothing was wrong.

"Seeing Dr. Coram helped me reflect on these invisible internal conflicts at a much more personal level. I came to realize, through my sessions with him at his office, that it was okay to acknowledge all these fears that I had inside me—and to just let them go. They might be ugly or uncomfortable when they came out—but once I opened up and let them go, everything became so much more beautiful and simple. Just by opening my mind to the idea of letting go—any anxiety or depression or fear or stomachaches (I used to make myself sick with all the anxiety and stuff) just magically seemed to disappear. And it went away immediately. It might sound ridiculous, but I found that just by being aware of everything that was going on inside me—the sickness went away.

"Actually, I have put a lot of those fears in the back of my mind. It might be interesting to go back and think about my experiences at that time. For example, back then if I got a bad grade, I would freak out. If I met a new person, I would automatically think that I needed to impress them. If they didn't like me, it meant that I wasn't good enough.

"I was afraid of new people altogether. I was afraid that I wouldn't open up, or I was afraid that if I did open up, they wouldn't like me. I didn't want to make any new friends. I thought that hiding these fears was the best way to take care of them. I believed that if I vocalized them, they would come true. When I could talk about these things instead of hiding them, it taught me that *my fears were just thoughts, negative thoughts—and I only needed to let go of them.* In my mind, I was thinking at that time that there were endless negative things that could happen to me. Dr. Coram really turned around my thinking. I began to see that there was actually a vast reservoir of endless positive things that could happen to me. I started thinking, *What if this person likes me? What if this person wants to be friends with me?* I became willing to try new things.

"For example, for the past a few summers I thought it would be really cool to get a job. But then I would think to myself, *Nobody would want to hire me—they wouldn't like me.* After working with Dr. Coram, I started questioning whether this was really true. Is it absolutely true that no one would want to hire me? So I had some job interviews and found out that every place wanted to hire me!

"As a result, I now work as a nanny for a lovely family with two children. I'm so lucky. I get to take the children to the park or to play every day. The children play with their friends, and I get to play with them. It's really a happy place to work. I truly feel that the universe guided me to where I work now, because the environment helps me to heal. Being away from Dr. Coram has been kind of difficult for me, but I have carried away so much— so much insight and so much wisdom and so much knowledge.

I was able to take that away with me when we moved back to California. Luckily we have been visiting Iowa once every few months, so I do get to see him once in a while. I'm really thankful for that.

"I had always wanted to be at peace with myself and with my highest nature, but usually I felt like I was in an argument with myself. Also I felt like I was moving against the flow of the universe. Even when my highest nature was trying to guide me, I just wasn't able to receive the messages—or make the correct decisions—because I was so consumed by confusion in my mind about my relationship with myself. Dr. Coram definitely helped me to open up a channel inside me—of direct communication with what is best for me—what my highest nature is pushing me toward. This allows me to make the most appropriate decisions for not only myself but for other people. And it also inspires me to do my best every day. Before, I would think, *Oh, it doesn't matter. I'm a bad person anyway.* Even though I tried to do good things, I felt like the universe, the world around me, would never support me. Seeing Dr. Coram opened up that channel to remind me that yes, the universe wants me to succeed, and the world wants to help me gain good relationships and good experiences—rather than feeling like everything was working against me and I wasn't meant to succeed.

"I'm back in school now and doing very well. I'm finishing up my tenth-grade year, after taking a year off, and I am going at an accelerated pace as fast as I can without really stressing myself out. I feel like what I am doing is enough, and I don't need to worry myself about doing more or doing better. Instead of comparing myself with other people—I am just focusing on being the best version of myself I can be. Now the anxiety just doesn't exist.

"There was a cycle in my thinking before I began working with Dr. Coram. If I had a negative thought, I was sure that for the rest of the day I would be having negative thoughts. Now, if I have a negative thought, I don't think I'm sentenced to have a whole day of negative thoughts. Really, I can change anything at any time. And another thing I notice that has changed is that I don't have a problem with my life being boring anymore. In the past, when I first saw Dr. Coram, I can remember feeling quite bored with subjects I was studying in school. I didn't go into his office and say, 'Look, I'm really bored with my schoolwork. Can you help me with this?' I didn't even specifically mention it. I just thought, *This is the way it is, and everybody has to go through being bored in high school.*

"But simply by going through the process of exploring different parts of myself—just by becoming more open and at peace with myself—my experience changed. Before, I might look at some subject in school as something I didn't think I would really need. But then I learned how to discover things within that subject that were actually exciting to me and could teach me things. Honestly, history is not my favorite subject. But I learned to look at it in a different way. I would study the people, not just the history and the dates. That helped me.

"On my job, sometimes I forget how lucky I am, and I'll get bored with it. But then I'll discover something new within the context of my job that I'm excited about, and I'll find a whole new passion there. In my day-to-day life, it is important to me to find even just one thing I am passionate about and focus on that. It never occurred to me before to explore my feelings by asking myself questions like: Is this absolutely true—that this job is boring? The process of self-reflection I went through with Dr. Coram opened my eyes to the habit of asking myself these questions—of looking more deeply into my thoughts and my feelings.

"The amazing thing is that even though Dr. Coram and I never discussed directly the topic of getting rid of the misery of my boredom—it happened. Automatically, completely on its own. I just opened my eyes more. Everything was already there waiting for me. I just wasn't opening my eyes to the vast potential richness of my life. I wasn't appreciating it before.

"Dr. Coram asked me earlier if I was ever somewhat reluctant or even afraid ... to explore feelings and thoughts hidden beneath the surface of my everyday awareness. And then on top of that, he asked me if I found myself feeling comfortable and relaxed about revealing my hidden thoughts in the presence of someone else. That's a really good question.

"I've thought a lot about that. I guess the atmosphere Dr. Coram creates in his office made me feel safe. He's not overbearing. I don't feel like he has expectations of me. He just holds the space for me. Anything I feel I am dealing with, or any internal monologue I am having—no matter what I say, he seems to react with love and acceptance. It really did encourage me to explore things. If at any time I got too deep into a topic, I could back out of it. The great thing about being with Dr. Coram is that very few times did I feel like backing out *of anything*. I usually felt motivated to deal with things. And another thought comes to mind. During my appointments with him, I always feel like I have as much time as I need. I don't feel pressured—like I have to rush to say what I need to say. I feel like I have plenty of time to explore what I need to explore. And whether I am talking with him or I am silent, it seems he is able to somehow know what is going on with me. He just goes into a healing state of mind and then is open to what I am saying and feeling. That makes me feel unusually safe, open, and free to explore my own feelings—and it allows me to find the courage to share those feelings with someone else."

In the beginning of the previous chapter, I posed a question: when our bodies stop working well for us (that is, when we get sick), how often do we think of "contacting the manufacturer?" I asked this question because contacting the manufacturer seems to be the most important step that I have identified—and that I have observed—in the healing process described by my patients. With this phrase, I am referring to the intimate and highly personal experience of connecting with one's larger, more expanded self—of contacting an inner, innate reservoir of wholeness that each patient talks about in their own way. Some refer to this higher power as God, or my higher nature, or Source, or any number of unique ways people find of pointing to something larger and more powerful than their everyday persona. Felicity made reference to *my bigger body of wholeness*. Elizabeth described accessing *a channel of direct communication with her highest nature*. And yet despite the profound transformation both Elizabeth and Felicity experienced in their day-to-day activities, neither of them considered their contact with a higher power to be in any way flashy or out of the ordinary. They simply described stepping up into a larger, more relaxed perspective—a bigger aspect of themselves. That more expansive platform allowed them to observe that the fear and negativity that had previously crippled them was constructed simply of thoughts and feelings—thoughts and feelings that they could choose to hold on to—or to just let go.

CHAPTER 8

A Sense of Relief—Pointing Us in the Right Direction for Healing

Relief is a symptom of healing. Most patients come to my office because they are hurting somewhere. They are sick or injured or broken in spirit. They want to heal, or to stop hurting, or to feel good about themselves. They want relief from suffering. Illness is a sticky animal. How do we treat it? Are we ill because we pushed too hard, or ate the wrong food, or contracted the wrong bug, or weakened our body through worry or pressure or bad environments? And if so, what do we do about it?

A sense of relief can point us in the right direction for healing. Usually a health problem is too complex to solve with just one approach. But if we feel relief, we must be doing something right. We can follow that sense of relief toward more relief until we feel really good. That's wellness.

Angela, a longtime patient, was asked in her interview why she kept coming to see me after the initial shoulder pain from her accident was relieved.

"I noticed at a deeper level, a systemic level ... emotionally, psychologically, and physically that things were happening that I don't even know if I have words for. I was starting to feel more like myself. Every time I walked into Dr. Coram's office, I had this sense of relief. What from, I didn't know. I had the sense that I was in the hands of a divine healer. Why did I know that? It's hard to say. It's how he touched my body, his incredible subtlety and his willingness to take my leg, my arm, my neck, or some part of my body beyond what one would think is possible, and I allowed it.

"Dr. Coram has helped me with a level of healing much deeper than my physical pain. He has helped me discover within myself the capacity to heal my lack of trust in the flow of life. I have let go of the tension I had felt for years that came from feeling that I was fighting for my life. I listen now to the voice that speaks from within my body, moment by moment."

Not surprisingly, Angela has noticed that this trusting, this listening—when she actually does it—stops the pain in her body before it begins. By being aware of what her body is saying to her, and by allowing her body to feel the relief of being heard and responded to, she can actually remove the root of pain and suffering before it takes hold in her body. She can stop the pain before it starts. Wow. That's worth learning.

Angela is energetic, strong, focused, and utterly playful. She is attractive and arrestingly fit, more like fifty than seventy. When she moves her right arm, the lower arm hangs loosely. The elbow section is missing.

"I have been seeing Dr. Coram for about six years, ever since a deer ran into the side of my car. The injuries from that accident triggered the pain and memories from a life-altering car accident in 1974. I had ninety broken bones in that first accident. I was blowtorched out of the car. Two of my main arteries were severed, and all my blood was gone when they finally got me out of there. I was dead. I'd passed over. It's a long, long story."

Angela summarized the story of her 1974 accident. She described being outside her body, looking down at the scene of the accident, and feeling that she had a choice to either proceed with the "death" or stay and deal with the massive damage to her body. When the ambulance arrived at the hospital, the doctors thought she was dead and had basically given up. Somehow she managed to very slightly squeeze one of the doctors' hands, and the doctors then turned their attention to very long, creative surgeries to try to save her life.

Angela wanted to describe how her overriding sense of her own conscious awareness remained lively and communicative, even though her body, by all common measurements, was dead. From inside that terribly broken body, she directed the doctors herself, telling them which parts of her body to attend to first so that she could live again. And despite the opinions of all her doctors that she couldn't possibly live (or walk, or speak) after such an accident, she lived and walked and spoke again. Angela continued with her story:

"Major organs were severed, liver severed and hanging outside my body. They tried to amputate my right arm (I've lost my right elbow), but I stopped them. The left side of my brain was smashed and damaged. It goes on and on and on. Lungs crushed, vocal chords, esophagus and trachea ripped out. So the fact that I am in a body at all is amazing. What sent me to Dr. Coram's office in the first place was another accident. I was driving late one evening, and a deer hit me broadside at the right side of my car and smashed it in. I didn't hit it—it hit me. I was on a main highway going maybe sixty miles an hour. I was alone and listening to the radio, and bam!

"Of course my original 1974 accident flashed before my eyes. I was shaken to my core. I went into slow motion, as we do, and I just kept going. I was in shock. The deer had ended up on top of my car, but I wasn't aware of that until later. I just kept on driving. It took me quite a while to figure out what had happened. I had my moon roof open, and from the corner of my eye, I saw some huge body spread over the car. It was such a big deer. I could see part of its head or its shoulders or something. If one of its big hooves had come in through the open moon roof, I would have been done in for good.

"I continued to the next town before stopping the car. The injuries resulting from this second accident led me to make my first appointment with Dr. Coram. When I came into his office, we looked into each other's eyes, and I immediately knew that he was a very deep guy. He was deep. This is what I saw. He was as deep *as I was willing to allow.* And I think he saw that in me right away. We connected on a very deep level that first moment.

"He started treating me by just putting his hands on my body and finding out what was going on, top to bottom, all the different areas. I remember him telling me, 'The pelvic region tells me everything I need to know. If I can get that completely flexible, if I can move that around in as many directions as deeply as it is built to go, then I know a lot about the rest of the body.'

"And most people are very frightened to move the pelvic area." Angela explained that our usual hesitation to treat the pelvic region is due to the kind of stresses that we often store there. "Lots of stuck energy, lots of stuck lymph, lots of fear-based stuff, because that is the area where you're your sexuality is. Because the pelvic region is also the base of the spine, it deals with the most basic impulses of survival, elimination and birth. To most people, it's a scary area. And Dr. Coram focused on that area first in treating me. I was very flexible from years of yoga practice and dancing, so he was able to move my limbs as if I was a gymnast."

Angela had used so many kinds of therapy to help her heal from the first accident that she understood how deep physical manipulation could facilitate deep healing, and she welcomed the stretching of her body to find its own extreme edge in order to help her body to heal. She remembered that I kept saying to her, "No one had ever been able to allow me to do what you allow me to do—so *you are teaching me*. Thank you for teaching me, for allowing me to learn so much."

"I was amazed at his openness. He's that, what, humble? He's that clear about the fact that both people are healing each other, both people are involved with this thing—both the doctor and the patient."

Angela kept emphasizing that deep mutual trust was the basis of our progress in the treatment room. That deep trust allowed us both to go deeply into the parts of the body that needed attention, places that needed a healing touch, areas that needed to be moved. She said, "Not only did I feel the pain, or the release of the pain, when he was manipulating my body; I also started unfolding the story of the trauma of the wound. You may not think they have anything to do with each other (the manipulation that the doctor is doing and the words that the patient is speaking), but they really do. And that's what is so cool about Dr. Coram; he's right on it. He knows that. He's listening to what I am saying while he's working on me, from that level." So what does this all have to do with relief?

"I have relief of pain for periods of time. Dr. Coram's work in the treatment room led me to the deeper realization that *any time I feel pain* in my shoulder, back, or hips, it is an accurate indicator of whether or not I am straining in my life—whether I am allowing myself to relax into the flow of life and let go.

"Here's what I began to notice. During the pain-free times away from the office, the place in my back would start hurting only when I started worrying. If I strained in any way, like worrying about my daughter or feeling pressured about getting a project done and I didn't have the time, that place in my back would start hurting like a hot poker, literally, and I could hardly stand up. And I thought, *Wow, isn't this interesting? Isn't this interesting!*

"What it said to me was that Dr. Coram was teaching me to bring myself relief by removing the very root of my pain and suffering. He was demonstrating to me again and again how I could stop the pain at its source by living a life without straining, without worry. So by listening closely to my body, I knew instantly when I had started to strain, and the pain worked like an alarm bell telling me to back off and stop straining.

"Now my meditation practice does that, too. But Dr. Coram has made it very obvious, physically. He was rendering me pain-free for long periods of time. And the awareness that that spot would start hurting only when I started feeling pressure from some behavior in my life was a huge breakthrough for me. It was a really important piece of information.

"I think the basis of my pressure and pain is fear. And fear is like a hot poker. Fear is some lack of trust in the universe. Fear gets you straining to do whatever you're doing on the level of will. Whereas if you trust life, if you trust the divine, if you trust that which is within you, then you will relax and allow nature to take care of it, whatever it is. You will allow the divine to work its magic; you will allow life to unfold as it should. But what happened to me as a human being (and it's why I had that big initial accident) is that I thought I could come in here and control life. I could come in here *and do it myself.* And isn't the whole purpose of life for us to learn to trust God? To trust the divine? To trust that which is our own intuitive guidance mechanism?

"If you don't trust *that* [the divine], then you are separated from it. Being separated from it, you've got to do it all yourself, and it's just overwhelming. When it's overwhelming, and you know you can't do it all by yourself, but you give it a big try, your body just takes the hit. That's why people get old, that's why people get sick, that's why people are in pain. It's the straining. It's not *Thy will be done*; it's, *My will be done. And I am going to do it, by God, if it kills me.* And it *will* kill me.

"So that is why I keep returning to Dr. Coram's office, even after the initial pain in my back was relieved. All those years of injuries. All that trauma to my body. All those wounded spots in my body that are still holding pain, still keeping me from being all that I can be."

Wounded spots within us that are not attended to can often become the *root of a new dis-ease*. Wounded, stuck pockets of pain and trauma kept Angela from noticing the actual moments when she was straining against the natural flow of life, when she was creating new experiences of pain and suffering for herself and for others. Angela's understanding and description of her healing process was so refined that I wanted to get her feelings about how the basic aspect of *intimacy* related to the whole healing process.

"Dr. Coram's choice of *Medical Intimacy* for his book title is beautiful, just beautiful. Intimacy, to me, is a willingness to be truthful with myself. To know myself well enough to be truthful about how I feel, what I want, what I'm willing to do and not do. When I am intimate with myself, I am not constantly fudging and evading and avoiding. So if I'm really willing to be intimate with myself, I'm willing to be spontaneous. And spontaneity is a result of my real trust in myself—my willingness to be free. Learning to be intimate with myself means learning to accept everything that I am, everything that's happened to me, everything that's changed, and everything I'll no longer be able to do, and then to truly accept how I think people see me now with all my injuries, all my woundedness, all my gifts.

"When some people read the words *medical intimacy*, they may not think of intimacy with themselves. The first thing that comes to their minds might be sexual intimacy. It's the one thing that Westerners are afraid of. *What does intimacy mean without sexuality?* Intimacy simply means that I feel free and unafraid with my partner—and so that whatever my partner, in this case my doctor, needs to do, I trust him to do that. We can't really go into this topic of intimacy without talking about spirituality. Why would any one of us be afraid of intimacy? The answer is simple. We are not *already* experiencing an intimate relationship with ourselves.

"If we are always distracting ourselves with drugs, if we always need stimulants to be revved up, if we always need to watch television, or to talk, or to have sex, or to run around in the car, that means we are afraid to be still. We are afraid to be silent. We are afraid to be intimate with ourselves. The fear is that if we are intimate with ourselves, we will find something we don't like.

"And yet, it is *only* when we go inward that we discover all the creativity, the fullness and the joy that cause us to want to do things—to dance and play and make our lives beautiful—to live life fully. Perhaps it is lack of exposure to an inward direction. Maybe our fear of intimacy with ourselves is just fear of the unknown. Our culture does not usually take the time to go inward. And we seem to be so very busy all the time.

"But I think it's deeper than that. All these addictions and distractions are simply because we have fear. We have fear, always, because we feel a sense of separation. We don't see others as ourselves. We don't see others as our family, as our world. We see them as something other than ourselves. So if we can spend time spiritually and emotionally to really get a handle on what that means to us—if we knew that when we look into the eyes of another and say Namaste, as they say in the Eastern cultures, that we are really saying, 'I recognize the divine in you that is the same as the divine within me. I recognize it and honor it. Thank you.' That's what Namaste means. And people don't go around in the East ripping their clothes off because they recognize the divine nature in each other. In fact, that's why they don't need to do that; intimacy means: 'I recognize the very core of your spirituality, and it's the same in both of us. Thank you for allowing me to see that in you.'

"So a doctor, a real healer knows that. A real healer is unafraid to see that divine nature in his patient and let the patient see the divine nature within him. And then we can really reach down to the place that needs to be healed, the place that has been wounded, the place that has been kept in the fear part of our life because it is part of the sense of separation. Together we can go to that place where we can say to each other, 'Good. I trust you, because we recognize that we are both divine.' Anything less than this is less than wholeness. Anything less will have some side effects. It's very simple—and that's who a doctor really is."

Note: Angela is now enjoying such robust health and successful body self-management that she has spent the fall and the winter playing on the beaches in Thailand.

CHAPTER 9

Fear—The Elephant in the Room

Nothing grips our gut with fear like the threat of cancer. It's a cultural thing. We all feel it. It's the elephant in the room that no one wants to talk about. A diagnosis of cancer freezes our whole world into a still frame. We're even afraid to call this disease by name. So we try to keep it at a safe distance by using a euphemism and call it the big C. Consequently, when we hear the story of a cancer patient whose oncologist tells her, "We don't know what is causing your cancer to go away, but whatever you're doing, just keep doing it," we smile. We cheer. The monster we all fear is being held at bay.

Beth is one of those individuals. Her story is the first of two we will explore in this chapter. With each of these patients, the monster of cancer within actually turned out to be an ally in disguise. Cancer—an ally? Strange as it may seem, the window of healing is often easier to locate when the situation seems dire. In fact, I actually prefer to work with patients who are facing life-threatening situations. In that moment of emptiness—when the fear of death from within freezes us motionless in our tracks—we have an opportunity to shift gears. To reevaluate everything about our lives and then alter our path. Fear is a great motivator.

And the momentum that fear creates can carry us into new uncharted spaces in our lives. What do we have to lose when the consequences for business as usual might be death?

Beth, whose cancer was so rare and aggressive that she had few alternatives available to her, chose to take the risk, opening herself up to something new to see what might happen.

"For the past three years, I've been battling a rare kind of cancer that just keeps recurring. Every year, it comes back. I've had both radiation and chemotherapy treatments, and they didn't stop it. Because my doctors in Omaha never see this kind of cancer, they referred me to the Mayo Clinic. Every three months after that, I got CT scans that were evaluated by the Mayo Clinic.

"On my way home from work, exactly one year since the end of my last chemo and radiation treatments, my doctor from the Mayo Clinic called me and said, 'The cancer is still there. It's back. It's in the lungs this time.' My doctor was up front with me. Because the cancer was buried so deep in the lungs, my doctor told me that they could not remove the tumors with lasers. They were going to have to tear my ribs apart and do this horrible operation. Probably I would also end up with a collapsed lung. I was devastated.

"The operation was already scheduled, but I still hadn't told my kids or anyone. Then about two days before the surgery, my doctor called me. She told me that the actual surgeon who was scheduled to perform the operation had said, 'You know, this cancer is so small. Why don't we just wait three months and see what it does?' Of course I felt relieved. I now had some space, some time. But I still had that agonizing feeling in my gut—*the cancer is still there. What is it going to do?* I still didn't tell anybody about the tumor after the doctor's call, but I did have to tell my boss at work what I was planning to do.

"Now here is the funny part. My boss told me that she had suffered from some health problems a while ago and she had gone to see a doctor in Ottumwa, Iowa—Dr. Charles Coram. He was unusual, she said, and I'd have to keep an open mind, but I should just try him. What could it hurt? After she explained to me that she had experienced nothing short of a miracle in his care, she urged me to make an appointment.

"So I drove twelve hours to Ottumwa, Iowa, to see Dr. Coram. My first visit with him was three hours long. I was amazed that he took so much time. And I hear that long appointments are standard for him. I mean, what doctor takes that much time with a patient, three hours to get to know you? During that first appointment, we discussed my fears and my worries. And by the end of the session, he was aware of any kind of problems that I was facing at the time. In following visits, we addressed the issues that were bothering me. These were some deep-down feelings that I didn't even think were a problem, but they were bothering me nonetheless.

"My husband and I were having some disagreements. Nothing big—we just didn't agree on some things. I don't like confrontation, so I just let it go. My way was always to keep things inside to avoid any kind of confrontation. Even with my friends, if I had a different opinion on something, I would just keep it to myself. In conversations with my husband—and with my friends—I would sit back and listen. Pretty much I would stay out of the whole conversation. But Dr. Coram told me that it's important for me to get my feelings out on the table. I remember him telling me what I needed to work on—and it wasn't really all that hard. For example, in my disagreements with my husband, I could just tell him, 'No, I don't want to do this.' I could stick up for myself, and it would be okay.

"It was a bold and uncomfortable step for me at that time. That was not the way I saw myself, and I certainly didn't think of myself as *that kind of person*. I didn't have much self-esteem, so I would hide behind perfect makeup and hair. At that time, I wouldn't even think of going out of the house without applying makeup and doing my hair. But Dr. Coram told me, 'You are beautiful the way you are. You don't need all that makeup and hairdo just to be acceptable.'

"Now don't get me wrong. Looking directly at my life and seeing what I needed to change wasn't easy at all. In fact, it was almost as scary as facing death by cancer. But with the support of Dr. Coram, and the memory of the ease and safety I felt in his office whenever I went deep into my own inner feelings, I found the motivation to try these new ways of being. Going into my negative feelings wasn't always pleasant or easy, but once I spoke them out, they seemed to lose their grip on me, and trying out new ways of being was easier. As a result, I now have a different attitude, and I don't worry so much about what people think of me. I just think to myself, *This I who I am—take it or leave it.* Beauty, I have come to discover, is not on the outside. Beauty is on the inside. So what matters most to me now is how I feel on the inside, because what is inside is *me*.

"It is not easy to change lifelong habits, and it takes focus. Changing the ways I thought about myself and how I interacted with others wasn't always comfortable, but I knew I had to do it. I remember that during those early days of seeing Dr. Coram, when I was in a conversation with anyone, I would visualize a little Dr. Coram sitting up on my shoulder saying, 'You've got to let your inner self express itself.' Believe me, that wasn't at all easy at first. I saw myself as the silent person. To express openly what I thought, in fact to say anything at all, was scary. But I found that when I did speak up, there wasn't a bad reaction from the group or from my husband. Now I find that when I am in conversation with others, if I have an opinion, I will give my opinion, and I add to the conversation.

"As a matter of fact, I have found new sense of interest in what I find myself saying to others. I often find that what I say is interesting not only to me but to others as well. That surprises me in a good way. And more than that—I can actually make people laugh. *This is crazy*, I think to myself. I've never done this before! This new attitude has changed my behavior in other ways as well. For example, in the past, if somebody else wanted to do something but I didn't want to, I used to go ahead and do it anyway because I didn't want to hurt their feelings. At work, they would ask me to do any little thing, and they always knew that I would do it, no matter what. In order to keep everybody else happy, time after time I would sacrifice myself and get all stressed out. That was hard on my body. But now I know I can't do everything, and I know I shouldn't overwork myself and get all stressed out. I've let go of the feeling that I always have to please others. I'll just say to my bosses and my coworkers when they ask me to do something, 'I'll do it if I can get to it.'

"To sum it up, I am unquestionably more open and opinionated. I let my feelings out now, and I say what I think with my family, my friends, and at work. Before, in my marriage, I let my husband decide everything. He made all of the decisions for the family. But now I openly voice what I think we should do, and I am an active part of the decision-making process. I have definitely changed.

"I still go in for cancer testing. But since I started seeing Dr. Coram two years ago, there has been no need for any more treatments. The doctors at the Mayo Clinic say, "We don't know what is going on, but whatever you're doing, just keep doing it." My body doesn't feel any different to me. I never felt the cancer in my body in the first place. It is more my mind and my soul that feel different. I am more open. I don't let things fester inside anymore. If I have something to say, I say it, especially if it's bothering me. I used to just absorb it, because I didn't want to bother anybody or make anybody feel bad. It still takes work. I still don't like confrontation. But I needed to take the risk of stepping out and voicing my feelings even if it might mean confrontation. I needed to do it, and I did it. And I am still doing it. I'm still working at it.

"After my first bout with cancer, I woke up. I used to be a worrywart. I worried about my kids. If my kids were having a problem, I felt it. When my kids were having a problem, I was having a problem. Now I definitely appreciate every minute I have to live. As I said before, I woke up since having cancer. And Dr. Coram definitely helped me do it."

The principle of healing that we see here in Beth's recovery is the process of turning inward—turning our attention 180 degrees to go deep inside the self. If we think of the body as the house that the spirit or the soul lives in—the place where our inner self resides—then we can use this analogy to understand the process of healing more clearly. So often what I see is that people believe that inside the house (that is, inside their body), there is something that might hurt them. It's like me standing outside my house and having a sense that there are monsters inside the house—monsters that are huge and might destroy me. But it's all make-believe. This belief is based on past experiences that really happened, of course. This fear didn't just rise up out of thin air. But fear brings up thoughts like: *I don't know if there's a fire inside the house, or if I might get attacked. I don't know what kind of monsters might be in there, how big they might be, or how dangerous they are. And if I look in there, the monsters might reach out and grab me—and then I might die.* The bottom-line fear is simply: *I don't know what is in there, but part of me has this fear that there is something bad in there.* The reason the patient's fear is so strong is that there is an underlying belief that goes something like this: *I don't believe that I have the strength or the capability of engaging with a monster who is that big.*

This house analogy is only a simplification to try to describe the thought mechanics that underlie the reluctance, the motivating impulses—of people holding back from going inside. I'm using this analogy to reveal even more clearly the subconscious reasons why so many people feel, *I'm afraid that there is something inside me that will hurt me.* The first steps of the healing process, the initial impulse that often allows my patients to feel safe enough to turn and look inside, are the simple words, "Let's go take a look." It might mean that we have to look at things hiding beneath our everyday activities, like shame or fear. We might have to look at conflicted feelings under the surface that are bothering us, like we did in Beth's case. But after that, in whatever way my patients find to go inward, at some point I will say to them, "Let's go take a look." Let's take a look at all these primary parts of ourselves. If you don't know what's in there, let's start guessing. Okay, so there are monsters in there. How many do you think there are? Let's get closer and closer and closer so we can look inside. Is there any way we can see inside that will give us more real information? We want that information so that we will know how to prepare, so we will know what to do to protect ourselves if we meet a monster.

And once many of my patients go inside, they come to the surprising realization that inside is nothing like they had thought it would be from the outside. Because we are all so concerned and afraid of these seemingly real monsters inside ourselves, our psyche says it has to be something huge. It has to be *huge* because I wouldn't feel this incredible fear if it was something small. But even those things that many of my patients observe and interpret as big, things they are sure are absolutely huge, are in actuality small. In clinical experience with hundreds of patients, I find that the most gargantuan issues are, ultimately, small. So the main way I help my patients like Beth is to remove the blocks, to remove the walls or whatever it is that stops that patient from going inside.

If the patient is in really bad shape physically ("I can't talk, or move my body, or feed myself, or even go to the bathroom by myself, and to me that's really *big*"), what if all the medical people and the doctors confirm to him that this problem *is* a really big thing? It's big and scary, and there is nothing anybody can do about it. That's the importance of the trust relationship that you have to develop with the patient. The doctors and the clinicians and the trusted family members and the caregivers are all the people who are helping the patient get closer to the window of his soul so he can get a better look inside.

If everybody else is saying, "No, it's horrible in there, and there's nothing you can do about it. You can't do anything at all about what is going on inside. It's out of your control," the patient will simply freeze up. The patient who wants to heal has to develop a trusting relationship with the people who have stepped up to support him. And they are the people who will help the patient to keep moving closer and closer to the window of his soul where they can encourage him by saying, "Let's look inside." Or at least, "If you are too afraid, you might trust me to go inside and look around. If you need some help right now, let's just hold hands. Then we can look in together."

Will this approach work as well with other cancer patients? I am glad to say that the answer is yes. This approach has worked in many other cases. In fact, I have four cancer patients right now getting similar results. Let me tell you about Todd.

One month ago, Todd was told at the Cancer Centers of America that he needed to start chemotherapy. His wife had contacted me right before that and asked me if I would work with him. Todd had contacted Cancer Centers of America in Chicago because the oncologist in Iowa City wanted to be so aggressive with his treatments. So Todd and his wife were concerned. They wanted a second opinion. The Cancer Centers of America use an integrated system that is open to alternative therapies as well as traditional. But when Todd and his wife went to Chicago to speak with those oncologists, they agreed with the Iowa City oncologists that his cancer needed aggressive treatments. They wanted to match the cancer's aggressiveness by attacking it at the same level that they saw the cancer growing. So they decided to do what Iowa City wanted to do. And then once they'd completed those treatments, getting it under control, getting it calmed down, getting it manageable, then they could look at some of the nontraditional methods of healing that they can do at Cancer Centers of America.

But Todd and his wife wanted to know if they could postpone the beginning of the treatments. They asked their oncologist, "Would it make that big a difference if we waited for a month to start this?" The Chicago doctors replied, "With the intensity of radiation and chemotherapy that we will be using, no, it wouldn't make a big difference. Waiting a month is not going to put us back too far." That's when Todd and his wife came back here. I worked with them for that month. I led them though the couple's process that I described in the end of chapter 3.

When they went back to Chicago and did a follow-up CT scan,

it showed that the growth had stopped. The doctors told them, "We don't want to do anything. Come back in three months, and we'll look at it again." So the diagnosis of the oncologists in Chicago went from, "We've got to do this right now. This is something very, very intense, very, very aggressive that we've got to be aggressive with," to, "Let's wait!"

After that positive feedback, they came to my office again. I saw them one more time. We talked. I said, "You will now have to continue working with these new ways of being [that we had developed during my month of working with them]—together at home." What I want to teach people is to become self-sufficient in themselves, not dependent on constant office visits with me. I want to help each individual patient understand that they have the power and the ability to heal themselves. I just offer my patients a brief opportunity to use me as a facilitator for their own journey of growth and healing. I am primarily offering them redirection. If they are ill or uncomfortable in their lives, I can reflect back to them that obviously they are off their path. All I need to do then is encourage them to get back on it, and then leave them alone. Really.

A scary, fast-growing cancer like Todd's is really difficult to turn around. Based on the experiences of the oncologists in both clinics, the cancer was very aggressive. They believed that this type of cancer would behave in this fast and aggressive way, so based on that experience, they would have to hit it pretty hard to discourage it. Some well-known doctors of alternative medicine in this country hold a different point of view in treating cancer. Since with modern chemotherapy and radiation we do attack the cancer, the cancer has a tendency, like any living organism, to become more aggressive. The cancer cells want to survive, and we attack them, which makes them say, "Hey, we need more people in our army, more cells, to overcome this attack." So the alternative idea is—let's come at it from a very loving, soft way and calm the cancer cells down. The cancer cells are all angry. They're all upset. They are trying to grow. We need them to calm down, calm down, calm down.

But this aggressive approach to cancer can be seen in the alternative medicine community as well. I have patients who want to attack their disease in the same aggressive way with herbs or supplements or alternative therapies. But the *feeling* underlying an attack mode toward any disease is *fear*. And attacking the disease from a feeling of fear does not create the atmosphere of calm and peace—of expanded, open, delicately honest self-reflection—which is so nourishing to the natural healing processes.

These patients express as much fear about the whole disease thing as about the traditional war-against-cancer approach. They see the disease as a scary monster and just attack it with a different medicine. They are still feeding the disease with fear in the same way. They're still attacking it. The disease cells feel any fear that we have inside us. They feel the fact that we want to destroy them. It's the same thing that any fearful approach is doing, but the methods, the tools might be different. It's not about what kind of approach we use. It's about the feelings that we have inside us when we use them.

So if a patient or a family member is pushing with fear toward any kind of treatments, I will often advise them just to back off for a while. To regroup. And to focus on giving loving support to the patient himself who has the disease.

In order to calm the cancer down, we don't resist it. We don't fight it. We don't attack it. We don't run away from it. And we don't ignore it. This is the dilemma we have dealt with for years when it comes to dealing with cancer. Some people react by saying,

"Oh, so you just want us to act as if the cancer is not there." My response is: "It doesn't matter if the cancer knows that I'm here. It's going to do what it's going to do." What I am suggesting is: Let's behave differently around a person with cancer. We have an awareness of the presence of the cancer, for sure. But the first thing that many people do when it comes to cancer is forget about the being, they forget about the person. At that point, the focus is only on the cancer. I tell them, "Now you're giving the cancer all of your attention. Why don't you give the human being, the spirit that resides inside that structure, more love, more attention, more compassion, and more warmth? You're giving all the attention to that darkness, that part that's destructive. And the person you love, the person who has the cancer in his body, is longing for the love, and the attention, and the kindness from *you*. He wants you to give *him* your wholehearted focus, to focus on *his* spirit, *his* being—to focus on the essence of *who he is*."

What I'm having Todd and his wife do is something new in their lives. So it's not like someone comes in with cancer, and I say to them, "Just keep on living your life in the same old way." Oh no. They *are* going to be doing things differently. But I don't want them thinking every day, *I'm doing this new thing differently because I'm treating my cancer.* Rather, I want them thinking, *This new thing that I'm doing is just better for my life and better for me.*

We're not just ignoring the cancer. We're not just pushing it aside. We're definitely, concretely doing something. We're changing the way we look at the cancer, though. And we're changing the way that we look at our lives in a practical manner as well. The thing I really love, in reference to what Todd and his wife are doing now, is that the steps they are taking to help balance Todd's health are actually enriching their life together even more. By doing the simple, loving couple exercise I taught them, they are forcing themselves to confront some things that they need to confront in their life. And they are enjoying the process. With patients who are going into remission, the overall mechanics of what seems to be working is that they turn their focus onto themselves. They start growing themselves and their lives in a much more fulfilling way.

In the process of helping someone toward creating a happier, fuller life, removing obstacles to happiness, obstacles to an integrated sense of wholeness in the patient, is the constant focus of my work. In Beth's case, she had little physical discomfort. Someone had to tell her there was a cancer tumor inside her. She had a small little symptom. And then the doctors looked inside and said, "We see something big and scary."

I try to keep my cancer patients away from focusing on their fears. I tell them, "The most important thing you can do every day is to do a scan on yourself. Look in the mirror. Look at your eyes. Really go through your body and your mind and feel yourself. How do you feel at this moment? Right now. If you feel good, if you are happy today, if you're full of joy, really you're good, you're good!" And that will overcome that internal destructive condition of the disease. It can't survive in that environment.

CHAPTER 10

Uniqueness—Finding Our Own Path

True healing demands that we be utterly honest and authentic. We are not talking about some quick fix where we take a pain pill to mask the pain. We are not talking about just addressing the symptoms of diseases and making them easier to live with. We are talking about real healing, where we dive down deep inside ourselves, locate the patterns that cause the imbalances that led to suffering in the first place, and then change them. How do we do that? The simple answer is that each one of us is completely unique, and therefore our path to healing is uniquely our own. We may be suffering from a cold, or a broken ankle, or depression, or colon cancer, but my cold is distinctly different from your cold, my depression is different from your depression, my cancer is different from your cancer.

That's why, when we come face-to-face with wanting to truly heal ourselves, we are compelled to refine our perception of truth precisely. Our own honesty, like a surgeon or a scientist, is then able to uncover authentic truth within us. This personal inner voice of truth will reveal to us clearly our own unpredictable uniqueness. Without any doubts. Personal uniqueness is surprising, full of uncharted territory and simple discovery. Uniqueness is playful and unfolds its true nature only by itself to itself. We can and will use assistance in this process of discovery. In fact, since we are by nature social animals, we often must. But the ultimate process of healing happens within us, and all our outside help is just to support the unfolding of this very personal inner journey.

Kate, one of my newer patients who is currently enjoying great strides of progress in her recovery, described her perception of these mechanics of healing:

"The main thing that I feel is that there is really no such thing as a healer; you can only heal yourself. Dr. Coram said something to me a few weeks ago that made complete sense. He said, 'Everyone is on their own healing path. There is no one path to healing. Everybody has to find their own way. The only thing I am here for is to assist you.'

"So for me, a healer is someone who creates a space, a container for me that is both safe and nurturing, so that I can go on my own healing journey.

"I started seeing Dr. Coram about a year ago. I had twisted my ankle while hiking in Colorado, so it made logical sense to make an appointment. (Dr. Coram is known throughout the region for helping his patients recover quite quickly from sports injuries.) But I knew when I made my first appointment that the real reason for seeing him was much deeper than a sprained ankle. For the last six years, I had been consumed with the process of healing from violent childhood sexual trauma. For most of my adult life, I had been completely unaware of any trauma in my past. But not blissfully unaware. To begin with, I have never had a successful, intimate, long-term relationship with a man. Except for one short affair that lasted only a few months, I have lived my life alone—never even dating. I am fifty-nine years old."

In her midthirties, Kate began to realize that she was afraid of men—but she didn't know why. And she couldn't figure out any reason she should be so afraid. For decades, she had suffered from depression and overwhelming fear and anxiety. Her fantasies were haunted by violence, and her nights were often sleepless since she had suffered from debilitating insomnia most of her life. When she was younger, Kate had spent quite a few years as a volunteer worker with a Buddhist group overseas doing charity work combined with long hours of meditation. But her meditation practices had been overshadowed by dark and violent fantasies of being tortured. More recently, Kate had been plagued by such self-destructive patterns of behavior that she had been barely able to support herself and was unable to progress in her career. Yet Kate radiates vibrant creative energy.

About sixteen years ago, Kate started her own business designing fabric art and unique women's accessories. She fashions her pieces from exotic fabrics hand woven by indigenous weavers from around the world, and she sells her work at craft fairs and local stores. Her business is just successful enough to pay her monthly bills. Kate basically lives month to month, as she has no savings. She knows she is capable of expanding her business much more, but fear, anxiety, and depression always hold her back. Consequently, her main focus for the last six years has been on healing the sexual and emotional traumas of childhood so she can stop feeling stuck in her life—and focus instead on developing her vast creative gifts. Hopefully, in addition she will find an opportunity to develop a successful intimate relationship with a man. Last November, Kate described the turning point in her life—the weeks when she first uncovered the hidden trauma that has disabled her for most of her life.

"When I was first getting into my art career, I started experiencing unbelievable fear. I would spend days just sitting on the couch watching TV, completely overwhelmed with the idea of supporting myself and putting myself out there. As time went on, I noticed that I was developing self-destructive behavior. If I needed to go to a craft fair early in the morning, I would be in a hotel room stuffing my face and watching TV until four o'clock in the morning, and then drag myself to the fair. I kept wondering why I was having such a hard time functioning. *What is wrong with me? Why am I so messed up?*

"Finally, I became severely depressed and suicidal. I was talking to all my friends and telling them that life didn't make sense to me. It hadn't made sense to me for a long time. I didn't know why I was here. I hated my life. I was depressed all the time. I seriously asked them, 'Should I kill myself? Is that a viable option?' I decided to do an inner journey. I sat down in front of what I call my spiritual altar and lit a candle. I used Native American herbs to purify the air and create a sacred space. And then I wrote, *Dear God, if you don't show me or tell me what it is that is keeping me from living to my full potential or enjoying life, I'm taking myself out.*

"After that, I lay down on my bed, and I had flash after flash of memories. I'd see myself in a crib with a hand coming toward me. I'd feel the closeness of a priest. I'd see myself when I was in in third grade, petrified in a bed with all these dark energies around me, all these weird flashes of impressions. When it was all done, I knew that either I had been sexually abused, abducted by aliens, or I had sold my soul to the devil. Well, I figured most likely it was sexual abuse.

"So I made an appointment for hypnotherapy. The first hypnotherapy session took a long time, but we got to a memory in which I was by the side of my childhood house and I had been attacked by a couple of neighborhood boys. A flash of memory revealed a clear image of what these boys had done to me sexually. Simultaneously I felt someone's hand grabbing my belly (a definite physical sensation), and then a rush of energy coming out of my belly as if something was being released.

"Feeling that graphic physical sensation followed by the energy rushing out of my belly was an indication to me that I was not making this up, that this was definitely an energetic something that had been stored in my body. So I thought, *Okay, I've been abused. This makes sense.*

"A month later, a second hypnotherapy session revealed further abuse. In the meantime, I was racking my brain to try and figure out exactly what had happened to me. I got snippets of memories. I consulted family and friends. But I knew that I only had a few of the pieces of the overall story. One afternoon, as I was sharing one of these snippets of memory with a dear male friend, he suggested that probably something more severe had happened than what my subconscious mind was allowing me to remember. He then described in detail what he thought had really happened. The minute the words left his mouth, I once again felt the physical sensation of a hand grabbing my belly, followed by a rush of energy exiting my belly. Next I felt a big smile appear on my face as if to say, *The truth is finally out.* I knew at that moment that my friend was telling me the truth.

"Following these revelations, on my fiftieth birthday, I was not in the mood to celebrate. Inspired by the insights I had gained from the conversation with my friend, I decided that I would commit myself to a sacred inner journey of self-exploration, and I would find out more details about what had happened. I locked the door to my apartment, sat in front of my spiritual altar, and again created a sacred space. Almost immediately, in my mind's eye I saw myself in a position, bent over my bed on my knees. I got into that position. I closed my eyes. I breathed into my body, and a whole flash of memory ran like a video though my brain. At that same time, I felt energy rushing out of my belly. Then I saw another position in my mind's eye. I got into that position, and the same thing happened. It was as if once the door was really opened, the process took on a life of its own and didn't stop. I barely ate. I barely slept. I drank tons of water. I was pretty much locked up alone in my apartment getting one memory after another for two and a half weeks."

Through this inward exploration, Kate came to realize that very severe sexual abuse by various family members began when she was an infant. There was another period of abuse by her priest, and then she was gang raped by neighborhood boys during her elementary school years. Kate continued to describe her journey of healing:

"Before in my life, when I would have sexual fantasies, they were always dark fantasies of being sexually and psychologically tortured. This went on for years until I thought I was really sick. When I started having memories of my abuse, all those sexual fantasies started to be explained; they were things that had actually happened to me. I was regressing and reliving the memories of real events in my life. As a result of all this revealing of past trauma, part of me experienced my whole world falling apart, but another part of me was relieved because my whole life now made so much more sense. I understood then why I had so much fear and anxiety all the time. The source of my debilitating insomnia also became clear to me. Many of the sexual assaults had occurred while I was asleep at night in my crib or bed. As the memories unfolded, it also became evident to me that some of my siblings were victims as well. I began to appreciate why they also have experienced so much dysfunction in their lives. Moreover, I finally understood why I was so afraid of men, why I had not had any romantic relationships, and how I had used my excess weight and the taking on of a more masculine personality to protect myself from the threat of any intimate physical relationships with men. I thought to myself, *Now that I know what is wrong with me, by the end of the summer, I ought to be healed.* My experiences of regression into childhood memories actually continued for three more years.

"But even after uncovering all these memories, my outer behavior didn't change significantly. I was still dysfunctional. So I thought to myself, *Now what am I going to do?* That's when I started to see Dr. Coram. In the first eight months, Dr. Coram helped me to release layers of resistance to receiving love. My inner talk as the result of my abuse had always been, *I hate myself, I blame myself.* In order to start receiving love, I had to dissolve the patterns of self-hatred within me and transform them into patterns of self-love. Part of the process of healing from abuse is that I realize that my life has been ripped away from me. Who I was supposed to be and who I became are two very different things. For example, I am a very affectionate and sociable person, but instead of getting married and having a family, I live alone and isolated.

"Repressed stuff is like a cancer. If it is not dealt with, the energy of it silently grows inside and finds ways to leak out. And then these parts of me that I had shoved away at an earlier time come back out and take over my life. I had adopted various patterns to cope with the trauma that I was carrying inside me. For instance, I used food to keep the memories down and hidden in my belly, and I also used food to cope with the constant anxiety and fear. I still comfort myself with food, and I still substitute food for love. Since I live alone with no husband or children to love and be loved by, I eat as a way to get love. Of course this backfires because all this overeating causes me to be down on myself and go into self-hatred, which is another symptom of the sexual abuse. As a kid, I blamed myself for what happened. I thought it was my fault. In essence, the coping mechanism of overeating brings me right back to my old familiar patterns of self-blame and self-hatred.

"It took some time to find my own healing path during my work with Dr. Coram. We have used many approaches that have helped. But at first I had the attitude that Dr. Coram was the healer, so I just sort of let him take over. And then, over time, I could see that I might have an idea and not say it because I was deferring to his authority. So we worked a lot on my being able to ask for what I wanted because we realized how difficult that was for me. For example, there was a session in which we were using therapeutic touch as a modality to help me have the experience of simply receiving love. I would just ask for whatever I wanted: touch me here, touch me there, and if that didn't work, I could change it.

"So I told Dr. Coram, 'Let's start with your hands on my feet.' After a couple of minutes, I wanted something else. But, oh my god, it was hard for me to ask for it. 'This is really hard,' I told him. 'I feel that if I ask for what I want, you are going to think I am a controlling bitch,' which was very interesting to me. I came to realize that embedded in the patterning I had taken on as the result of all that abuse was the feeling that *I can never get what I want. I can only get what somebody else wants.*

"In that particular moment, Dr. Coram simply stated, 'I can tell you that you are not a controlling bitch. But if ever you are, I can promise you that I will tell you. If I don't say anything, you can presume that you are not.' Through that one session, it became easier and easier for me to ask for what I wanted. Then

I started working on letting go of that pattern in the rest of in my life, simply by asking for what I really wanted. I kept asking myself, how am I going to start asking for what I want when I am with this friend, or with that friend? But more and more, I am doing just that, and as a result, I'm feeling happier in my friendships.

"Knowing how hard it is for me to sort out my own inner feelings at times, I inwardly wonder how Dr. Coram was able to structure an environment for me where I felt safe enough to access the delicate nuances of my own personal preferences and desires, a healing space for us work with each other that was safe enough and nurturing enough to allow me to open up to my most vulnerable feelings.

"When you go to see him, he is extremely present. By present I mean right there, listening to every word. There are no distractions. You can tell he is not somewhere else. He is right there, and nothing else exists at that time. Where I am at, having someone who is extremely present is very important. It gives me validation so I can tell my story and know I am being heard. Presence and attentiveness. Yes, that's the core of it; presence and attentiveness combined with love. I just feel much loved by him, and understood. Just that alone is extremely healing. And what do I mean by the word love? Isn't the feeling of love obvious? I remember in those first months, it was just a feeling of relief knowing that I had someone I could go and talk to. Someone who was going to give me what I never got at home as a child. Someone whose eyes were going to light up when I walked into the office. Someone who was going to be genuinely excited to hear what I was going to say and who was willing to go with me wherever I needed to go emotionally. Someone who was willing to be there with me and not just talk but willing to really experience it with me, the heartbreak and the love, all of it.

"It is important that more of this healing ambiance gets infused into other medical environments where we go for help. Part of it is to get doctors to realize that there is more than pathology involved. Doctors should realize that pathology is an end result of many things, and you've got to deal with the things that led to that pathology.

"I just recently had a hysterectomy. How did I get that? It's very clear to me that my female organs are where I stuffed all my memories. When I got my first memory of sexual abuse with the hypnotherapist, I saw myself—in the memory immediately after the assault when I was left alone—take the memory of what had just happened and shove it down my throat into my belly. I could taste it as it went down. And then I remember thinking, *I can't tell anyone about this*, because of the threats that had been made about what would happen if I told anyone. So I shoved the entire event down into my belly as a way to forget it.

"I definitely think that if I had been able to uncover and release the trauma that I swallowed down earlier in my life, I might have been able to avoid the hysterectomy. The main thing is—a doctor has to first realize that there is a whole story that led up to this present illness. He has to be willing to find out what the story is and then listen. And that has been one of the most healing things for me—just to have someone who is not in a rush, who doesn't have an agenda, and who is interested in really exploring, *Who is this person? What makes this person tick? What happened to this person?* When someone is really interested in what I have to say, their love is the healing element. That, I think, is the most important thing. That is why Dr. Coram is so successful, because his patients feel loved when they are with him. There is no judgment. There is genuine interest. He meets them right where they are. And for all of us, I think—being met, being seen on a deep level is extremely important.

"I want you to know that I'm definitely not finished with the healing process. But I have great hope. I'm still wild, I'm still overeating, and I'm still overweight. I still have the remains of coping mechanisms, but I'm not letting them get me down. I'm not having the cycles that I used to have of going nuts and then lying down on the couch for days just watching the TV without brushing my teeth or showering. If I do stay up late and pig out, I'm not down on myself like I would have been in the past. 'You idiot,' I used to say to myself. 'You're doing it again! You're never going to improve. What's wrong with you?' That's not happening as much anymore. I'm more loving to myself now. Now I tell myself, 'It's okay. I've done it again, but I am healing. It's not my fault I am this way. I'm healing from posttraumatic stress disorder. It may be slower than I like, but I am getting better, and I will continue to get better.' That is a major change because the root of my old distorted self-patterning was self-hatred.

"I managed to let go of the self-hatred with the help of several things. First, by putting the blame where it belongs—not on myself but on those who assaulted me. Secondly with self-forgiveness, huge waves of self-forgiveness. Until recently, my mantra had been, *I hate myself … I hate myself*. Now, more and more, my mantra is, *I am healing, I am getting better, I love myself, I love myself*. In fact, I'm starting to have moments while working when I find myself singing, and I am happy. Now that is *rare* for me. Most days I still have to force myself to get through the day. But I'm having more afternoons, or a day here and there where I feel, *Hey, this is fun. I like being alive! This is fun!*

"I'm becoming more productive, and I'm developing new

skills with my artwork. My anxiety is less, and I'm feeling less fear. I'm not having a lot of suicidal thoughts. Maybe that's because I notice each day that I'm focusing more on my positive thoughts and giving less and less attention to my negative thoughts. Best of all, I'm beginning to see what being able to take in love is all about—that is, feeling safe enough inside to actually receive love. And I am beginning to get a sense of what that is going to mean to me in my relationships and in my life. The walls of resistance are coming down. I've got a way to go yet, but I can feel what's on the other side, and I can feel what it might be like when my walls come down."

CHAPTER 11

The God Finder—Tying It All Together

Interviews can be compelling because they are real stories about real people. And if these stories resonate with us as truth, we can learn from them. By learning, I mean the kind of deep insight, the aha moments that can lead us toward actual inner transformation, insights that can help us shift our whole way of being toward greater harmony, balance, and peace.

The reason I gathered these interviews for this book is that I wanted to reveal, through the stories of a variety of patients, the delicate steps of healing. The stories are all unique, yet one experience is central to all of them. Each patient described the importance of creating a safe space—a space where they felt supported enough to open up to their deepest feelings, a space where they could explore their inner terrain without judgment, without fear, and just see for themselves what was inside. They used this sacred space to open themselves up to a new and more intimate relationship with themselves and with others. And their dis-ease, which at first had seemed to be a monster about to devour them, in the long run gave them an opportunity—a chance to grow to be more in love with their own lives.

The question that naturally comes to mind is, how do we

recreate the healing process documented by these stories for ourselves and for others? How do we infuse into our own lives a more nurturing space for healing? How do we help each other heal? Recently, during a patient's visit with me, I greeted her at the reception desk with a warm smile. "I've got it," I said. And then I just looked at her, my silent attention communicating more effectively than any words.

"I'm a God finder," I told her softly.

My patient contemplated the concept for a while and then responded, "Yes. I was wondering what the last chapter would be about, and that's perfect."

I then began to explain to her what led to this realization. I told her that I have been working with a patient who is facing the threat of cervical cancer. We have been working together to support her healing for months. During that time, she has been connecting more and more deeply with the essence of her being.

I am referring here to the same precious essence that has been identified by all the deepest teachings on our planet—the deepest reality within all of us and everything that is. And when that essence is drawn out from within so that it can be seen on the surface level of our lives, we all experience something sacred. We know it when we see it. The sacred essence of being is both familiar and divine. Most cultures, both scientific and religious, know it as God.

I noticed that while this patient was talking with me, she went through a shift. The divine essence became so predominant in her appearance that when I looked her, I saw God shining through her. I saw her radiating her divine essence.

One of my patients recently told me, "When I believe something, I feel it in my body." This statement clearly tells us why we gradually become whatever it is we believe, not just in our ever-flexible minds but also in our bodies. It's an automatic process. Our innermost thoughts give rise to feelings that manifest themselves as a concrete, flesh-and-blood reality in our physical form. So if we come to feel through our inner exploration and inner knowing that we are part of the wonder of God, if we begin to see ourselves as a mirror of the divine, as a player in God's plan for the universe, then our bodies will reflect that knowing spontaneously. And this transformative process is going on all the time.

My sense is that this God-self within each of us is drawn out of us when it sees the God-self in others.

If we get caught up in attending only to a person's physical being, if we only look at or work with their dysfunction, then we give away our God-ness, our God space, because God doesn't see that. He doesn't see in that person just an illness or a disability or a broken body. We need to see beyond that person's individual problem and look directly at the whole, amazing, powerful soul that each person really is, and then we will be in our God space. And that's what draws the God-self out of the others around us.

We are all familiar with this tendency to be naturally drawn toward the more charming and subtle levels of experience in our everyday lives. For example, when we see someone we love dearly, someone we have connected to deeply in the past, we approach them with an eager, open heart. We are irresistibly drawn to them. If we have enjoyed a really rich and intimate relationship with them, we feel an even more intense attraction to them.

But the relationship we have with our own innermost self is even more intimate, more compelling, dearer to us than any of our outer relationships. So when we allow ourselves to expand into that sacred inner space, we are in our God space, and we will naturally draw that same quality out of the other people around us.

A lot of times, we can't be in that space. We are running around the house, or at work doing the things that we need to do. We are more in our flesh and less in our spirit. But choosing, when we are able, to favor this deeper way of seeing is both possible and practical. It's just a matter of shifting our priorities.

What we need on a daily, ongoing basis is a depth of connection with ourselves and others. If we have that depth, if we feel that deep connection, we will care for each other in a more loving and sensitive manner. It happens spontaneously without thinking much about it. It's just an innate, natural response we have when interacting with those most dear to us. We can see it in our personal relationships. When we are connecting on a deep level with people we are close to, we care for them better.

If we stop caring for each other, we're going to create more distance. But when we limit that distance, and we start to feel a deeper connection and closeness, we're apt to do more for the other person. We're actually less selfish in that space. We're protective of that closeness, that delicious intimacy with another. We like that feeling. We want to stay there, and we're willing to do the right things to honor that connection so that we can experience more of it.

Also, if we have that deeper intimacy with ourselves, we are more likely to care better for ourselves, both our outer self and our inner self. And if we have that depth of connection within our everyday lives with everyone, then chances are we're going to take better care of each other, look out for each other more, and stop all this exploiting. Yes, if we actually felt a depth of connection with everyone, all the corruption in our world today would stop.

So the exploitation and the corruption in our society are really just symptoms of the inability of people to fulfill themselves in a more satisfying way.

In my clinical practice, as I described in chapter 4, I found that there are two different methods of helping people—mood-making experiences or transformational experiences. Mood making is when we are only affecting people on the surface. Transformation is when the experiences go all the way through, creating a shift in the whole person, heart, mind, and body, by connecting the person with his soul. Transformation is deeper.

If we are just making sure that someone's physical needs are taken care of, that their basic needs are provided for, that is just the outermost materialistic level of care. But it's not enough for a being who is truly a spirit housed inside a body.

So we must get way beyond this interaction that we have with the body. The body is, in a sense, just a way of moving the spirit around in the physical world. In the physical world, we need a physical body to allow that spirit to interact. That is all it's there for. And sadly, so often for many people, it's all we really see. This focus on the level of the flesh exclusively has overtaken the current medical community, causing many parts of Western medicine to lack that transformational depth. All they are putting their attention on are the physical things, and the reason they are ineffective is because they are not affecting the depth. That's all. They're not going where they need to go.

It's like trying to stop car accidents by improving the cars and ignoring the drivers.

So there are just a lot of body shops! Unfortunately, that's what's going on in our medical system today. Western medicine keeps coming up with better ways to deal with all the horrible things that people do to themselves. We know it's ineffective, and it's because we are not getting to the source. Now we are functioning in our society at a level of exploitation. We can't afford it anymore. We need to have another means of currency, or something has to change, because right now there's not enough money to counteract the effects that people are having on themselves.

The thing is, a person who has been sick for a long time has dug himself into such a deep hole of dis-ease that just changing some of his beliefs is often not enough to pull him all the way out of a life-threatening situation. He can't dig himself out all alone. He needs the energy and help of others to reach out to him and help him up and out of his deep hole of habitual and usually unconscious self-destructive behavior patterns.

In order to heal on a transformational level, this person needs the combined effort of all the modern and traditional healing resources working together on his behalf. That's why we call this approach to healing integrative medicine, because it integrates all the resources we need to heal, whether physical, psychological, or spiritual.

So to sum it all up, as I said in my introduction to this book, the most fundamental step in the process of healing is for each of us to connect more fully to our true inner selves. How do we do that? It's simple. I believe the opportunity to connect with ourselves more fully is present every day. Here is how it happens.

Through the ordinary day-by-day events of our lives, other people that we encounter—usually people that we already love and respect and admire—will reveal to us a piece of our true self. We might refer to it as "I felt valued by that person," or, "Someone saw something in me that I never knew was there," or "No one has ever mentioned anything like that about me before." That admired person recognizes something in us. Something strong, or fine, or talented, or whatever. But something *big*—something big to us. The magic comes when that part of us actually *hears* what they say and sees it to be true Then that deeper part of us will automatically step out further into our lives—and that deeper *big* self will become part of our *daily* self.

But what I believe happens (sadly), over and over again for people, is they miss that. They miss that opportunity that is happening on a daily basis.

From my perspective, the time to really go for exploring the true self is when we are younger, when the world has not yet suppressed our true self—to any great degree. Young people are constantly chomping at the bit to come out of their constraints. They are trying to express themselves. They are trying to be, trying to do. And then, by their society or by their elders, they are being told no, that's not appropriate right now—that's not allowed here—or whatever. That constraining attitude suppresses the young person's exploration of their true selves.

But in my case, I was fortunate as a youth. While I had just a very tiny handful of people say, "I see something in you … something *big*," for whatever reason, the true self within me accepted what they said *as true*. I didn't mistrust it, and I didn't doubt it, even though at the time I didn't understand it at all.

Remember the story I told you, in the introduction to this book, about my meeting with the travel agent in Galveston, Texas? Let's revisit that story again as an example of how we might open ourselves to the opportunities that life presents us with to connect with our true self—or not. I was a seventeen-year-old boy at that time, with nothing to support me—no resources, no fancy education, no stable family. And somehow, I don't know how, I came up with this odd idea that I wanted to go to Europe after graduation. At that very moment, I could easily have said to myself, "That's crazy. You can't do that. It doesn't make any sense. It's impossible." For whatever reason, I was fortunate enough to not even question if I really wanted to go to Europe. All I remember is that I said to myself, "All right, I'll go in here and talk to this travel agent ..."

And what about the effect on me of the unspoken attitudes of the other actors in my story? For example, if that travel agent had known that I had no financial or family support, she could have said, "I've got other things to do. I don't have the time to waste because this is not a *possibility* for you." I was very fortunate that she accepted that *I thought it was a possibility*. And since *I* thought it was a possibility, *she* thought it was a possibility. Looking back, I know now that I was only there for *that* experience. It was that simple *willingness* that I had to just go with my impulse ("I want to go to Europe")—my *willingness* to just step out and take some simple action, that was the catalyst for me to place myself in that completely new environment. It wasn't about going to Europe at all. It was about stepping into a new level of possibilities for myself, a new level of being.

So often when these voices inside of us—angels, God, whatever you want to call it—share with us a desire, an interest, to step forward into something big and new, we allow our habitual pragmatic mind to step in and question our innocent desire. But it is just these innocent desires, these simple, spontaneous feelings of interest that can most easily lead us into the discovery of the deeper part of ourselves—our true selves.

My vision is that we, as a people, begin to work with the children of this planet—both the children in our lives and the inner children in our hearts. How do we do that? Through deeper and more intimate relationships with both—both with the children and with our own personal inner child. As a result of that deeper intimacy, quite naturally, we will begin to connect with each other—true self to true self. Once connected, my vision is that we make sure that *at that moment, at that moment of awakening,* during *that experience—when the true self shows up*—that the true inner self gets *to stay out.* We do that by assuring the true inner self of our children and our own inner child that indeed we see it as *wonderful* and *loving* and *supportive.* That way, we will all become attached to that way of being. Because as we know, the things that we become attached to become our world. We all know that.

Made in the USA
Lexington, KY
26 May 2017